The Sword, the Serpent, and the Spiritual Realm

The Sword, the Serpent, and the Spiritual Realm:
A True Story of Supernatural Power Over Evil

By Salad Vang

Purpose House Publishing

Copyright © 2023 Salad Vang. All rights reserved.

Cover design by PurposeHouse Publishing.
Published by PurposeHouse Publishing, Columbia, Maryland.
Printed in USA.

No part of this publication may be reproduced or distributed in any form or by any means, or stored in a database or retrieval system, without the prior written permission of the author.

PurposeHouse Publishing, www.purposehousepublishing.com

The publisher is not responsible for websites (or their content) that are not owned by the publisher.

First Edition: August 2023

ISBN: 978-1-957190-12-9

Unless otherwise indicated, all Scripture verses are taken from the King James Version (KJV), which is public domain.

Scripture quotations marked (AMP) are taken from the Amplified® Bible, Copyright © 2015 by The Lockman Foundation, lockman.org. Used by permission. All rights reserved.

Scripture quotations marked (NIV) are from the New International Version, Copyright © 1973, 1978, 1984 by Biblica.

Scripture quotations marked (NKJV) are taken from the New King James Version®, Copyright © 1982 by Thomas Nelson. Used by permission. All rights reserved.

Dedication

I dedicate this book to my Lord and Savior, Jesus Christ. He is the Lord of Heaven's Armies—companies of angels with swords who execute His Word. He has taught my hands to war, and I am forever grateful.

Contents

Acknowledgements ix
Chapter 1: The American Nightmare 1
Chapter 2: The Saving Power of Jesus Christ 11
Chapter 3: Strange Days 19
Chapter 4: The Roller Coaster 27
Chapter 5: Home Invasion 41
Chapter 6: Dream Training 51
Chapter 7: More Miracles, More Persecution 61
Chapter 8: New Territories, New Levels 71
Chapter 9: Foolish Things 81
Chapter 10: Many Nations, Manifestation, and Miracles 91
Chapter 11: Fruitfulness and Pandemic Healings 105

Acknowledgements

Writing and finishing a book is no small endeavor. The experience is both challenging and rewarding. I especially want to thank my wife and the other individuals who helped make this happen. Thanks to everyone on the Purposehouse Publishing Team who helped me so much (www.purposehousepublishing.com).

CHAPTER 1: THE AMERICAN NIGHTMARE

He threw the first punch, and the men in the hallway burst into a drunken brawl. That is how the night ended but not how it began. I had left the office feeling unstoppable. Finally, I was living my dream life. The night was going to be great.

"You are the last patient for the day—hope you are feeling better. We're all done, Mary."

"Thanks, Dr. Salad. So what are you doing tonight? It's the weekend."

"Haven't you heard? Everyone knows about it. The famous Hmong comedian Xab Thao and his partner, Chia Yang, came all the way from Thailand to do a concert in Ohshkosh tonight. Aren't you coming?"

"I've been busy working seven days a week. I didn't know about it."

"All tickets and booths are sold out, but if you do come, let the security guard come get me, and I'll let you in."

"Alright, I'm coming then."

"See you tonight, Mary."

"Okay, bye, Dr. Salad. See you later."

Mary left the clinic, happy about her newfound concert information and personal invitation. I headed for my office to change before leaving for the concert. I was "on top of the world." Driving

110 miles per hour without a care, I zoomed past every vehicle in sight. The concert would solidify my success and status in the community—I would be unstoppable.

When I arrived, everyone swarmed. Like bees flocking to honey, admirers surrounded me, including the staff, volunteers, band, makeup artists, and the Hmong stars preparing for the show.

"Wow, great concert, Salad!" the clan leader grinned. "You sure do know how to throw a party, man."

I smiled at the compliment and raised my glass to clink his before swallowing a shot of alcohol. "This is just the opening act, my friend—the real action starts when you see Xab Thoj on that stage." Reclining in the convention center's premiere VIP table, our shot glasses were immediately refilled by a clan leader from Madison, Wisconsin.

"How on Earth did you pull this off, Salad? I mean . . . Xab Thoj! Just about every important person I know has tried and failed to bring him to America." What my friend said was true. I had succeeded where many others had failed, and this man would know because he was a Hmong clan leader.

"I suppose it helps to have influential friends," I replied cryptically. "After all," I continued, "here I am, talking to a clan leader. Who can refuse me a small favor?" We laughed heartily and clinked glasses again. My day had been filled with many similar interactions, and I had been told by numerous people this truly was the best and wildest concert they had attended.

I felt a hand on my shoulder and turned to see my friend Johnny. "Salad, it might be time to upgrade that beast of a V12 supercar you're driving."

"An upgrade? It's worth a hundred and thirty thousand dollars! Why would I upgrade a new car?"

"Well, maybe you can buy your dear wife a new car if you're still happy with yours. I just locked in an advertising deal that is sure to land me a lot more business, and in turn, I will be sending even more business your way in the week ahead. And I mean a *lot* of business!"

I laughed again and beckoned the clan leader. "A shot of liquor for my friend Johnny here! Let's celebrate." The clan leader poured Johnny a shot and stepped back as the six of us raised our glasses. "To even more business!" I smiled.

"To an endless stream of business!" Johnny laughed, and we all clinked our glasses and shot the liquor.

The rising young Thai star had just started a song we both knew well. I had sung this very song on one of our recent Karaoke evenings. I ran a busy clinic but always found time to party with the Hmong celebrities, Wisconsin local leaders, and government officials I had befriended. I understood all too well how crucial influential relationships are, so I always found time to socialize, letting my friends know I was ready to play hard after working hard.

We would party from Thursday to Sunday but sometimes started the drinking and carousing on a Wednesday evening. I would party with the local leaders, and the mayor would often visit one of our houses, where we would sit together, eating exotic food and drinking fine liquor late into the evening. Alcohol was crucial at these parties, and we drank with a purpose. Karaoke evenings were also a hot favorite among our well-known friends and associates.

Johnny turned to me with glazed eyes—he had been drinking all night steadily, as we all had. "The cases are not special, Salad, but the *people* are." He rubbed his thumb and forefinger together with a smile. "They're all people who are highly insured!" We laughed uproariously, and he clapped me on the back before making his way to a table filled with snacks. Within seconds, an elegant, middle-aged woman struck up a conversation with the men around me. A moment later, her warm, tinkling laughter could be heard throughout the VIP section. People are attracted to laughter, and we were soon joined by a successful Hmong businessman I had met at a recent dinner.

Watching Johnny's graceful interactions with this eclectic range of dazzling VIPs filled my heart with pride—our family had achieved a high-echelon social standing. Within one generation, we became doctors and lawyers and succeeded in businesses. Coming to America from a poor, third-world country was a dream come true. My family fought alongside the U.S. government against the spread of communism from 1962 to 1975, and thousands died while protecting U.S. interests. The North Communist army invaded Laos in 1975, so my family fled to Thailand via an American cargo plane, and we were placed in a refugee camp. My father had already passed away at that point—he died in 1973, leaving my mother to fend for herself and her six sons. I was five years old when the communists took over, so I had a good understanding of what it is like to be starving, sick, or poor. Under brutal communist rule, the people live hopeless lives, and there is no one to help them. However, that all changed for us when we arrived in Chicago, Illinois, in 1979.

A waitress filled my glass yet again, and as I held it out to her, I shook myself free of these distant memories. It was good to know I would receive more patient referrals from these clan leaders and friends. My family and I lived in a big house in Michigan, and some of our Hmong friends had commented it looked like a castle. In my opinion, it was just a normal house, and I didn't really need a bigger one, so I considered what else I could buy to make my wife happy. We were already living "the high life" and eating only the highest quality foods. I would spend one or two thousand dollars on a bottle of liquor without thinking twice, so I was hard-pressed to find a suitable outlet for the extra cash rolling in. *Maybe I need a yacht?*

I surveyed the leaders and wealthy business elites surrounding me, and at that moment, I felt invincible. We were American citizens, living the American dream and rubbing shoulders with some of the most influential people around.

I felt a sense of deep satisfaction at everything I had accomplished. That is until I looked across and happened to see a solitary figure in the corner of the VIP box. A sudden unease came over me when I saw my wife sitting in a chair alone, drinking only tea and appearing to . . . pray? It annoyed me that she had recently started behaving in this neurotic manner reminiscent of her childhood faith. But it also saddened me that our life no longer brought her joy. I quickly looked away to the waitress—she was waiting with a smile to pour more alcohol for us to drink. I wondered if I should go easy, as my head was beginning to swim, but I figured I was here to enjoy my big moment and not dwell on this one glitch in what I thought was my perfect life. Besides, too many people wanted my attention.

The young star finished her set, and the stadium erupted into a deafening chorus of applause, cheers, and whistles. A hush fell over the crowd when it became evident Xab Thoj was about to walk onto the stage. I wanted to sit back and fully enjoy the show I had organized, but problems were beginning to develop. As Xab's set was about to begin, a worried-looking head bartender approached me. "Mr. Vang, I hate to have to tell you this, but we are running out of liquor. We are almost out of everything, so we have moved some of the cheaper liquor from downstairs up to the VIP floor."

I was extremely surprised to hear this, even though almost everyone at the concert was drunk. "What do you mean? Did we not discuss stocking copious amounts of alcohol? I told you how I expected people to drink!"

"Mr. Vang, we had three times the amount of stock on the premises than we have ever carried before. The people are just insatiable."

I laughed at the disbelief I saw on his face. My people knew how to party! "Jim, you must arrange to have more alcohol delivered! Quickly, make a call, and bring in more from anywhere before the people notice."

"Yes, sir. I will do so immediately."

The head bartender scurried off, looking more worried than before we had spoken, but within forty-five minutes, he informed me the extra stock had arrived. We were back in business! Xab Thoj mesmerized the crowd; they were hanging on his every word.

I stepped into the hallway to talk to a leader from another town when I first noticed two men waving their arms in animated conversation. I could see they were both drunk because they were staggering as they flailed their arms, but I had no idea their exchange was about to turn violent. I was too far away to hear what they were saying. Suddenly, one of the men threw a haymaker punch, knocking the other man into a group behind him. A split second later, a bystander jumped forward and punched the man who was still standing. He dropped to the ground like a sack of wheat. Then, it was like watching a chain reaction as more people got involved and more men started dropping like felled trees.

The fight would soon be contained and squashed by the ample security I had hired.

The concert enabled me to attain the status I desired from those I considered important. I earned a lot of money and gave plenty away, but I was usually strategic about who I gave to. As an atheist and secular humanist trained in evolution principles, I knew where and how I should succeed. Despite my ups and sometimes humorous and crazy downs, I still believed I had life figured out.

I truly was living the American dream. My private practice was booming, I was rolling in money, and I had many influential friends in high places: Hmong celebrities, the mayor of our town, local leaders, doctors, lawyers, and even congressmen. I wore only the best suits and shoes and stocked the most expensive liquor. I was drunk on worldly success and my proximity to power. It appeared I was on a never-ending winning streak.

The one thorn in my side was my wife Tsee's newly resurrected devotion to her primal, neurotic faith. Despite how many gifts I bought her, the fine dinners we attended, or how much money our bank accounts showed, Tsee grew increasingly unhappy with our lifestyle. She claimed to feel hollow and unfulfilled, but how or why, I couldn't understand. It was true I was a raging atheist, totally against the concept of the existence of a God, so for me, this was as good as it got—and it was pretty darn good by my standards. My brain, grit, and shrewd business skill had gotten me where I was, so I was a vehement non-believer and refused to allow Tsee to befriend any believers in Christ other than her mother.

I just knew it was poison to the intellect. Tsee, however, would not deny the experience of her childhood. She claimed the life was draining out of her, believing she sensed some grave danger approaching . . . so she started praying constantly and seeking her God. At first, I was tolerant of her reasoning, trying to understand what was wrong, but Tsee couldn't quite put her finger on the problem—she said she just sensed something terrible was happening. I shrugged her comments off, believing I was somehow allowing my sense of guilt to seep out and Tsee was simply picking up on it. I would have to be more stoic. I couldn't allow this to sidetrack my focus on the business growth that was about to take place.

But something was about to happen. I was too focused on business and social status to see it.

***

"Hey, Salad!" a sultry voice called out. I was floating on a huge inflatable swan in my pool and looked up, but I couldn't see who was calling my name. "Over here, Salad . . . I'm going to hop the fence so we can chat." It was my neighbor. I watched as her torso glided above the fence—she had obviously just stepped onto a platform. Her agility greatly impressed me as she hoisted herself over the fence and spun deftly to land on her feet. She wore a very minimal pastel-pink bikini. She adjusted the bikini top straps, and I smiled, knowing it was for my benefit.

Who am I to complain? I smiled to myself, but my eyes swiveled guiltily to my own house, knowing my wife was out shopping. My neighbor clearly also knew my wife was out.

"Hello, Jong. That's quite a bikini."

Jong held my gaze as she casually lowered herself to the pool edge, allowing her legs to dangle in the warm water. "I was tanning, and I heard you splashing around, so I figured I'd come to invite you over for a drink." She looked pointedly at the large whiskey tumbler I held in my hand.

"Why not pour yourself a drink from that cart over there?" I offered. "Or there's excellent champagne in the bar fridge if you prefer?"

Jong smiled mischievously, then flicked her long braid from her shoulder to her back. "Well, the truth is I actually want you to see the new king-size bed I've just had delivered to my room." She adjusted her bikini straps again.

I raised my eyebrow and gave her a wicked grin.

My grin was about to change . . . my American dream would soon turn into a nightmare.

On several nights, somewhere between 2 a.m. and 3 a.m., thick, dark clouds would momentarily drift apart, so the full moon could reveal the slim silhouette etched against our house's wooden fence. The figure was motionless as if cast in stone, eyes rolled back in the head, with the lips muttering something incomprehensible. The bright moonlight revealed a feminine form arrayed in a splendid, colorful coat. She wore a traditional Hmong outfit of red, black, blue, green, and white—delicately woven into an ornate design, but the scene was far from beautiful. The woman was zombie-like, standing with her arms outstretched, muttering and chanting.

Suddenly she lowered her left hand into a pocket of the colorful coat and retrieved some kind of magical charm, which she then held aloft. Her mouth began chattering a new incantation. She became animated, the volume of her chanting increasing and falling, the cadence reaching a near-hypnotic rhythm. She reached into her other pocket, pulled out a handful of soil from the local cemetery, and held it to the sky.

The venomous words slithering from her mouth were unidentifiable yet horrifying; clearly, the dark forces she summoned to seduce men possessed Jong. The rhythm of her incantation suddenly slowed, and her voice dropped back to a whisper. She held her left hand aloft with the charm, then brought her right hand to the left, rubbing the grave soil into the amulet. She opened both palms to the sky, then blew the dust into the air toward our house. She turned again and again, repeatedly blowing fragments of matter into the air as she turned to face each of the four compass points. Instantly thick, thunderous clouds started rolling toward our house from all four directions as if summoned.

The dark, malignant magic and the monstrous demonic entities the witch conjured would soon change our lives forever.

"What good will it be for someone to gain the whole world, yet forfeit their soul? Or what can anyone give in exchange for their soul?" (Matthew 16:26 NIV)

The Lord supplies for all those who willingly yield to Him. He gives them a completely different mindset on success and happiness in this life. In Christ, real success is marked by one's willingness to sacrifice to God and, hence, follows with immense promises of blessings.

CHAPTER 2: THE SAVING POWER OF JESUS CHRIST

"Silence! Be still!"

The man standing in the boat commanded the raging storm with power and authority. Instantly, the wind died down, the waves slowed to gentle swells, and a great calm fell upon the sea and the men in the boat.

Wow! Who is this man? Tsee wondered, her eyes glued to the TV—transfixed by this powerful man who could calm a storm just by speaking to it.

Tsee was fascinated. The man had been sleeping at the back of the boat with His head on a cushion when His disciples woke Him. With a loving grin, He shook His head at them, then stood up and shouted at the storm . . . and it stopped. Tsee had never witnessed such awesome power in her nine years of living on Earth. Although the film she was watching was a documentary, in her young mind, she was convinced this man was still walking the Earth. She desperately wanted to meet Him, and the longing in her heart raised many questions. *Where is He? I want to see this man. I want to meet Him. What country is this . . . where the wind and the waves obey the voice of this man?*

Once the movie had ended, the pastor who had shown the film as an evangelistic tool spoke some words that changed Tsee's life—he said, "If you want to receive Jesus today, say this prayer with me." Tsee fully believed what she had seen on the TV, so she immediately repeated the prayer with him. She wanted to meet this man, so she naturally accepted Him as her Lord, although she wasn't really sure what that meant. As the youngest sister in the family, Tsee figured someone would explain it to her.

She was eager to attend church from that day, but her family members were not yet believers. Tsee's adopted brother, who was older than her, had started seeing into the spirit realm regularly and was terrified because he believed he was under demonic attack. He started attending church on her mom's advice—the Hmong Alliance Church in Akron, Ohio, where Tsee grew up. He would pick her up almost every Sunday to go to church with him, and she loved every minute.

It was only much later my wife realized the Lord had called her as a little girl. He chose her and had a specific purpose for her. And once Jesus' love has touched you, it is only a matter of time before it completely transforms you. It took another three years before Tsee's parents converted to Christianity, after which the entire family began attending a Baptist Church. Life was good.

I first met Tsee in Madison, Wisconsin. A relative suggested I should meet her. So when she was visiting her cousin, I suddenly appeared out of nowhere. She seemed instantly taken with me. She later told me she liked my powerful presence and thought me extremely intelligent. So that was the beginning of our romance. Unfortunately, or fortunately, perhaps, Tsee's family did not have deep scriptural teaching, so the fact that I was a fervent atheist was not much of a dissuasion to her. The cultural pressure to marry a Hmong man, especially one studying medicine and, according to Tsee, who was also so charming, far outweighed my absence of faith.

Back then, there were no Internet or cell phones, so we developed our relationship by writing letters to each other almost every day, posting them by mail. We occasionally called each other on the phone but never really talked for long because it was expensive back then. They were long-distance calls because I was still studying at university, so we only talked briefly. Even though we were both still going to school to earn our degrees, once we had grown closer, we decided to get married.

Even though I was still studying chiropractic and medicine in Portland, Oregon, Tsee said I was a good husband then. She felt loved and cherished, and even though she was studying and working too, it felt like we were working toward something together, supporting each other. We hadn't gone out into the world yet, but for two young students, our relationship felt right. That, however, would not last long.

When I had completed my degree, we moved to Michigan, where I started my first clinic in 2002. Before long, I began making good money. And not long after that, I was making astonishingly good money. Soon after, Tsee began noticing some changes . . . my personality was shifting. We were involved in the various Hmong communities in our area, and I began to spend time with some powerful people for business purposes. I became increasingly less tender and no longer behaved like the loving husband Tsee had once known. Instead, darkness had come over me. Tsee felt she could no longer reach the loving man she had married.

In June 2011, Tsee had a life-altering experience. After a long day of cleaning and cooking, she laid down to rest for a few minutes before I came home. She quickly fell into a deep sleep and began to dream. She dreamed Jesus visited our house and was sitting on one of our living room chairs. The moment Tsee saw Him, she knew it was Jesus. The man who had calmed the sea was before her—her powerful Lord! So she ran to Him. She fell to the floor before Him and started crying as she put her face on His knees. He put His hand on her head, and even though He was patting and comforting her, she simply couldn't stop crying. Tsee didn't understand why she was crying, but her tears kept flowing. She could feel how much Jesus loved and cared for her, and the comfort He brought to her soul was like a fountain of crystal-clear water in the middle of a barren desert.

Suddenly Tsee heard a vehicle turning into our driveway—it was me—I had just arrived home from work. Her heart began to pound. Panicked, she cried, "Jesus, you have to leave now! My husband has just come home, and if he were to see me crying, it would make him angry. He would not allow it." While she spoke those words in the dream, the Lord disappeared, and my wife woke up.

Intuitively, Tsee knew Jesus had appeared to her for a reason, so she started questioning herself. *What's happening to me? What's going on in my life? My marriage? Where am I now, and where am I headed?* She also knew her relationship with her Lord had dwindled—it had become virtually non-existent. She felt lost. However, she did recognize the Lord was revealing something important to her. He was telling her there was something very wrong that she had to address. She felt compelled to do something, and her dream of Jesus comforting her was the start of her questioning. She began seeking the Lord in earnest. She started praying again, deeply wanting to spend more time with Jesus.

We were about to find out why.

"Mom, Dad, something's wrong with Emily . . ." Our second eldest daughter's eyes were full of fear. Intense fear.

"What do you mean," Tsee asked, a pang of dread seizing her. "What's wrong with Emily?"

Our two younger daughters exchanged a glance; then Elaine replied: "We don't know. . . she's shivering, and she is terrified of something." Tsee and I sprang out of bed and went to Emily's room. When Tsee saw her, she immediately realized what Elaine meant.

Emily's entire body shook violently, and my wife had never seen her so horrified. She had the blanket over her mouth and nose, and her eyes were darting around the room crazily.

Then I burst into the room. "Emily, what are you afraid of?" I barked.

"There are shadows at the door, Dad. Two shadows." Her eyes darted from the door to the window, and she spoke again: "Now they're over by the window! Two shadows." The pure terror in my child's eyes was harrowing. Emily's eyes darted back to the door, and with a note of hysteria, she shrieked, "They're coming! They're coming for me!" I was frozen. Nothing had prepared me for this. Suddenly Emily turned her face to the left, her back arched and her chest pushed up, her eyeballs rolled backward, and she began convulsing. Foam started dribbling out of her mouth.

About a week prior, Emily had told us she was having headaches like she'd never had before. I thought they might be migraines or perhaps that my daughter just had a lot going on, causing her stress and tension. The Friday before, however, Emily had said to Tsee she was scared. Very scared. She said she had seen strange, frightening things, and Tsee could tell she was highly unnerved. My wife had gone to her room to talk with her, and initially, Emily said she was feeling better. But she was still shivering, and she seemed unusually afraid. She kept saying she saw spirits. At that point, Tsee didn't believe spirits could possess our daughter. That Sunday, April 14, 2013, Tsee and I learned a terrible lesson.

When Emily began convulsing, we called 911. When the paramedics arrived, Emily was still experiencing the seizure. They administered some medication and took her to Saint Elizabeth Hospital, about five miles from where we lived. They did a computerized tomography (CT) scan at the hospital, followed by a magnetic resonance imaging (MRI) scan, but then told us they did not have the expertise to help Emily. Then, they took her to the children's hospital in Madison, Wisconsin, about two hours away. Tsee and I followed the ambulance.

Emily ended up staying in the hospital for a month. The doctors treated her for epilepsy and found a virus in her brain that caused an infection. They performed a spinal tap, and after comparing the results with those from Saint Elizabeth Hospital, they began treating her with a huge amount of medication to overcome the virus. The medicine, however, almost killed her. Before long, her kidneys were functioning at only fifty percent due to the stress of the medication.

After spending a week or two in the Intensive Care Unit (ICU), doctors transferred Emily to a regular hospital room, but the seizure activity quickly started again, and they moved her back to the ICU. They added more medication to her treatment schedule, after which she started saying strange things, like how she'd seen the other side. She claimed she'd seen angels and had seen Heaven. She even said she wanted to leave and go to Heaven. Tsee began to pray earnestly, pleading with the Lord to spare our child. From that point forward, Emily began to recover, growing stronger each day. The Lord heard my wife's cry. He had once again calmed the storm.

During this time, there was a very helpful hospital nurse, and it seemed he was sent from God. He kept quoting scriptures about Emily's survival and encouraging Tsee to have faith—even if only the size of a mustard seed. So Tsee kept trusting the Lord, and Emily continued recovering . . . but we began to realize she had suffered a severe loss of memory, and her motor skills had also greatly deteriorated.

Emily couldn't remember who she was, and she no longer recognized us— her parents. She didn't know her age or siblings' names. Thankfully, a few days before the hospital discharged her, she started remembering a few more things, but she lost her long-term memory. She couldn't remember things that had happened a few hours or days ago and was talking like a five-year-old child. It was heart-shattering.

We could finally take her home, but she had to take medication constantly. It was tough because, as our eldest daughter, the entire family was used to her fulfilling important responsibilities in our home. We now had to take care of her and the younger ones, and with Emily no longer able to help them learn, it was pretty rough. If she turned the stove on, she wouldn't remember to turn it off again. Or she would bake cookies but would have no memory of baking them.

By Fall 2014, Tsee was desperate. She remembered her dream and started fervently seeking the Lord about the way forward. In her heart, she knew the way we were living was not right—drinking and associating with ungodly people, even if it would have made us millionaires. It was not a healthy lifestyle—it was ungodly, and my wife couldn't bear to live like that anymore.

After being released from the hospital, Emily never had another seizure, but she also took her medication regularly. Her motor skills began to improve, but nowhere near the level they had been previously. She was bed-bound most of the time, unable to walk properly, and sometimes crawled because her body was weak. It was as if the skill set she had acquired throughout her life had been radically reduced—skills such as mathematics and reading had deteriorated appreciably.

While Tsee and I were praying for Emily one night, the whole room became bright, radiant, and holy. We saw two angels whose appearance was whiter than snow enter the room. They were so tall we could only see from their shoulders down, and each held a golden sword downward, pointing its tip toward the ground. And these swords were not made of regular gold—it was a gold so pure we knew it was not of this world. The angels stood in the middle of the room. Suddenly, two dark shadows about three feet tall came out of Emily's body, went into the drywall, and disappeared. The angels also disappeared, and Emily was completely healed. She sprang from her bed and went to talk to her siblings. Her memory was wholly restored, and she spoke with them with excitement and joy. It was a miracle.

Jesus had saved her from epileptic seizures, a brain virus, and a deadly infection, making her whole again. We had seen the saving power of Jesus Christ through my wife's prayers.

"I am the gate; whoever enters through me will be saved. They will come in and go out, and find pasture. The thief comes only to steal and kill and destroy; I have come that they may have life, and have it to the full." (John 10:9-10 NIV)

Jesus makes a bold proclamation. He declared himself the Good Shepherd and promised the believer who comes to Him salvation and the fullness of joy. He will faithfully protect and guard us if we trust Him and do not lose hope and faint (Psalm 23). Jesus Christ declares that life becomes abundant—it continually increases and is strengthened in those who do not rebel against Him. Today, do not rebel, but truly follow Jesus, the tender but strong Shepherd who guides us through life. When we believe in faith and greater confidence in Him, it will lead us to the fullness of life because His Spirit within us, who gives life, will empower us.

CHAPTER 3: STRANGE DAYS

Tsee hummed as she headed for the massive third-floor bathroom. As she looked at its swimming pool, she froze...

Three enormous, dark hyenas were scrambling out of the pool, nails scratching on the tiles. The beasts were as big as grizzly bears, and Tsee, knowing they were flesh-eaters, instantly understood they were there to eat our family. They were going to crush our bones and tear us apart. Tsee yelled downstairs, screaming that I had to help her. There were two doors—one opened from the bathroom into the hallway, and the other was an exit to the balcony. The doors were opposite each other in the bathroom, so she told me I must close the door from the hallway to prevent the sinister creatures from leaving the bathroom.

Tsee could not go through the bathroom to shut the balcony door, so as soon as I held the hallway door closed, she quickly ran downstairs. Tsee could hear the hyenas cackling and clawing as they tried to break through the walls. There was a hill next to our house with an enormous oak tree, so she assessed the situation and immediately knew she had to break off a branch from the oak tree. Once she had broken off a branch, it lifted her into the air—as if it were a balloon—and she started flying. She flew over to the balcony, and as she reached it, she saw the hyenas dashing madly toward the balcony door. Tsee was terrified—she knew they would maul her, so she was too scared to approach the door to shut it. She turned to her left, seeing two people on the balcony next door to our house. It was our neighbor and her son, but for some reason, the son—a teenage boy—looked like a little child. Seeing them gave Tsee the courage to shut the door because she didn't want the hyenas to attack them. As soon as Tsee had shut the door, she woke up.

It was an extraordinarily vivid and terrifying dream. I calmed Tsee down, telling her it was only a dream, but she was very disturbed. She believed the dream had some specific, sinister meaning. I told her dreams meant nothing, but I knew she wasn't convinced.

I also noticed a change in Tsee's behavior, but in my ignorance, it only annoyed me. I was having the time of my life mingling with the popular people and business entrepreneurs, making more money than I ever had dreamed of, and it bothered me that my wife was constantly trying to reign me in. Around October 2014, my wife was constantly praying—even more than usual, fasting more. Unknown to me, she had been truly born again. She had even been taught, by the Holy Spirit alone, to pray in the Spirit, and she had become spiritually awakened. During this time of fasting and prayer, she cried out to God and began to hear His voice more clearly.

However, every time she entered into a fast, the intense spiritual attacks would increase—sometimes in her mind with self-doubt, other times in her dreams, but more often, she was targeted in the flesh. Her obsession with religion deeply bothered me, and I began verbally attacking her. I would tell her she is no good and everything she does is wrong. "Even your cooking is no good," I would shout. "Other women are better than you."

It was very difficult for her to hear me saying these terrible things, so she fasted and prayed more. At one point, Tsee had been fasting for four days. I came home that day and told her she had to accompany me to visit a friend, but she didn't want to go. She knew it would be another drinking party, but I insisted that she accompany me. I left the house, expecting her to be ready when I returned, but she had reached her wits' end.

I was unaware of this at the time, but as the time approached for me to arrive home, my wife was praying on her knees in the living room, crying out to the Lord, saying, "God, I can't go on like this anymore. I've done everything within me to pray to You for a resolution. Are you true to Your Word? Do you really care for me? Do You even love me? Lord, I really don't see the fruit of Your love in my life. I am struggling to believe that You truly love me."

Suddenly, my wife heard the Lord's voice deep within her heart, then resonating through to her mind. "You say I don't love you? Do you remember that day, the day I saved you?" Tsee was silent, not understanding what the Lord meant. Then He continued, saying, "That day, it was I who saved you. I was standing right behind you, and I scared that man off." In a rush of revelation, that incident from all those years ago suddenly made sense.

It was a cloudy fall morning in the ghetto of Akron, Ohio, and Tsee was walking to school early. She was about ten years old, and no other person was in sight. Tsee knew she was about to die! She also knew her loved ones would never find her body, and her family would never know why or how she had vanished. She was looking up into the face of a tall, slim, Caucasian man who had piercing blue eyes and thick blonde hair. The man had driven his car into the driveway on the sidewalk ahead of her, blocking her way forward. Her eyes glazed over with a mixture of fear and resignation as she stared into the man's cold blue eyes—she knew she was powerless to defend herself but had a chilling sense of his wicked intentions. He reached out with both hands in an attempt to grab her. She froze with terror.

Suddenly the man's focus shifted. He took a few steps backward, staring at something behind Tsee. Whatever he had seen behind her had overwhelmed him with fear. He took a few more steps backward, ran quickly to his car, cranked the engine, and peeled out as he sped off.

Tsee remembered. Her Lord had undoubtedly saved her. Instantly, she knew how much He adored her. Tears welled in her eyes, and where frustration had once been, meekness, humility, and love flooded her soul. "Lord, I'm so sorry. I never once considered it was You who saved me that day. Oh Lord, I realize now You are my true

Father, and You are the only One who truly loves me. I know now who I am."

Immediately, Tsee's faith increased, so she prayed again:

Lord, I am so grateful for everything You have done for me. I now know that I am Yours, and You are mine. I believe in Your Word. Your Word is active and powerful. Thank You, Lord. I believe that this man I married—Salad Vang—is a man of God! He is a disciple of Jesus Christ. This man will serve You all the days of his life and has been chosen to do Your will. He will obey You. He will climb or descend any mountain for You, and if You ask him to cross any ocean, he will do it for You. You will never find any man more willing to do Your will in this moment. You chose the apostle Paul from among the multitude to carry Your will to the Gentiles, and now You have chosen this man to extend Your will into all the world. I believe this with all my heart and everything within me. Thank You for sending Your angels to help in setting my husband free and setting our home free.

I could see something different in Tsee's eyes. Something had changed. She was more resolute—but even more accommodating toward me. The guilt I felt angered me even more because I knew I was doing wrong, even betraying my wife and family with my sin. I relented from my usual harsh ways for about a month. But one night, I arrived home after work and was adamant that she accompany me to my favorite karaoke club. My wife had made herself clear. She never wanted to go to any nightclub ever again—but I didn't care. She had no choice.

When we arrived, I walked over to my friends at the bar and ordered a round of drinks. I began joking and laughing, glad to let off some steam from the workday and spend money like it was water. Tsee clearly didn't want to be there, so she left to sit in the karaoke room. Knowing we were going to the karaoke bar, she went prepared. She pulled a Christian worship CD out of her purse and pushed it into the slot on the jukebox.

She selected the track from her custom CD from the menu and pressed the play button. Still, the track that started playing was not from her CD—it was presumably one of the party tracks from another CD in the jukebox. Tsee tried switching it back to the CD she had chosen, but none of the buttons worked. She stared at the machine, wondering what was happening, but it still would not respond when she tried again. She unplugged the jukebox. When she turned it back on, she opened the track slide to see if there were any other CDs in the machine, but there were no other CDs in there except for hers.

Tsee realized something wasn't right, and that's when it happened. In front of her, just to the right of where she stood, a shadow of a humanoid form walked past. Suddenly, she heard a voice hiss, "What are you doing here in this place? This place is not for you. Don't ever come here again."

All the hair stood up on Tsee's arms and neck. She knew this was a demonic force. Whatever it may have been, her presence bothered the entity, and it claimed the karaoke club as its territory for the works of darkness. Suddenly the Spirit of God arose within my wife. She remembered the scripture that says the Lord is with her and He is her *sole* protection, so she knew the spirit could do nothing to harm her. Instantly the spirit disappeared. Tsee took a deep breath, then started singing her song of praise to her God.

A short while later, we began to prepare for Thanksgiving. I love Thanksgiving. The clinic was closed for several days, and it was the perfect opportunity to drink with my friends. And it didn't stop at the holiday. Two days after Thanksgiving, on November 29, 2014, I was invited to a late celebration. A Hmong leader from Wausau, Wisconsin, had arrived to celebrate Thanksgiving with a group of local Appleton leaders and other influential people from the surrounding area. As soon as we arrived at the bar that evening, the men started drinking beer, talking, and eating—a huge pork roast was the main dish. My wife was uncomfortable, and I could have sworn she was praying under her breath, but I was enjoying myself too much to worry. The celebration soon reached a fevered pitch, with everyone doing shots, drinking beer, and making toasts. I was raucous in the festive atmosphere when suddenly, icy-cold fear gripped my entire body.

I stared behind my friend, my eyes wide as dinner plates. Shadows were moving near the wall. I rubbed my eyes. No . . . they were creatures . . . weird, humanoid-beast chimeras moved out of the wall, snarling and with pure evil intent in their eyes. I thought I might be drunk, but I knew I could drink way more than I had, and I had never experienced anything like this while drunk.

I sat stiffly in sheer terror. All around me, these horrific creatures appeared—tiger-human hybrids, monkey-human hybrids, and various other animals I recognized mixed with a warped human form. Some creatures were small, some were skinny, others were fat, and some were rippling with muscle, but all had grotesque, deformed faces with terrifyingly wicked eyes. I could barely move; I was so scared, but I watched as an ape-like creature drifted through one of the Appleton leaders and breathed a dark green fog into him. That seemed to make the man drink more heavily. Then I saw a deformed tiger-humanoid creature do the same to a woman sitting to my left. Her eyes instantly darted around the table, searching for another drink.

Suddenly something pulled at the back of my jacket. I whirled around to see what it was, but nothing was there. So I turned to my wife and said, "Come with me to the bathroom real quick."

She frowned but nodded and followed me as I got up and almost ran from the table. I closed the bathroom door behind us, and Tsee quickly said, "Let's go home." She was surprised when I immediately agreed with her. She looked at me intently and asked, "What's wrong?"

"I'll tell you at home," I replied, taking Tsee's hand. I pulled her to the side door and sprinted toward the car as soon as I got to the parking lot. My wife trailed behind, taking off her high heels to run after me. She didn't know her prayers had already caught up with me.

"Howbeit this kind goeth not out but by prayer and fasting." (Matthew 17:21 KJV)

"For our struggle is not against flesh and blood, but against the rulers, against the authorities, against the powers of this dark world and against the spiritual forces of evil in the heavenly realms." (Ephesians 6:12 NIV)

The spiritual realm is a reality. The real battles and fears we confront are not flesh and blood—they are spirits. Our real enemies are Satan and his dark spiritual forces hidden from the physical realm. These evil spirits, called demons, reveal themselves in a person's carnal thoughts and worldly desires. They give terror, cruelty, and oppression, which lead a person to pursue self-fulfillment that births sins. Satan and his demons are doomed for the lake of fire at the end of the age. But for now, they are dangerous threats we must fight and defeat. We cannot war against these demonic activities with earthly weapons. Our best offensive weapons are to stand firm in God's power and put on the full armor of God, loaded with the aid of the Holy Spirit, the Word of God, and prayer.

CHAPTER 4: THE ROLLER COASTER

I arrived home shaken to the core. I pressed the remote to close the garage door but felt unsafe—even behind locked doors. Still seated in the car, I turned to my wife: "Tsee, I'm afraid. I never want to see anything like that ever again!" Tsee put her hand over mine and smiled as reassuringly as she could. "Please help me," I pleaded. "What must I do? I must know those monsters cannot get to me. I never want to see them again." My wife then told me all about Jesus as we sat in the car in our garage.

She assured me Jesus could save me and protect me.

I took everything she said to heart, but the experience completely exhausted me. We went inside, and I closed all the blinds and covered up any crack of a window that might allow a demon entry into our house. Eventually, I flopped onto the bed and managed to fall asleep.

When we woke the next morning, the first thing I asked was, "Tsee, what can I do to be saved? I'll do anything!" Tsee had been praying for this moment for years. A loving smile crossed her face as she touched my shoulder, "You must give your life to God, Salad. You need to repent for your sins. You know now God is real, and God's enemies are real. You need to ask God for forgiveness, and you must also forgive everyone who has ever harmed you. You must commit your life to Jesus completely." I desperately wanted to give myself to God. If it meant He would protect me from those monsters, I was all in. I also knew deep inside I could not continue living the way I had, but I didn't know what ritual to go through or what prayer to say to give my life to Him.

"But how, Tsee? What must I do?"

"We need to simply thank God for His saving grace, my husband. We must worship Him on our knees." I immediately grabbed her hands and kneeled on the bed next to her. Tsee began leading us in prayer, and a strange warmth enveloped my heart as I repeated her words. I grew up believing crying was not masculine, so I was surprised when I realized hot tears were falling from my eyes as my wife prayed. Suddenly the room was filled with a bright, radiant glow as if Heaven had opened a portal into our bedroom. It shone down onto our heads, filling the room with a glorious presence. We both saw it and were stunned—it was unmistakable, and even though it was warm and bright, I was still shaken by what had happened the night before.

"What's happening, Tsee? Where is this light coming from?" I was scared, but somehow it was a reverent fear, nothing like when I had seen the demons—that was terrifying. My wife was silent, offering me no answer.

I didn't know it then, but Tsee had sent a silent prayer to God from the depths of her heart, "Lord, this is your chance to come into this man's life and manifest Yourself in him." Tsee knew God had answered her prayer.

While we held hands, praying with our eyes closed, pure white radiant light inundated the room. This light wasn't the only confirmation of God's presence; I also felt the room washed with such an abundance of pure love, unlike anything I had ever experienced. I had no idea what was happening, but at that moment, I became silent. This powerful love was washing away my fears. Tsee softly began to thank God and praise the name of Jesus, and when I heard His name, my mind began to feel calm and completely at peace. I had never felt such peace, love, and tranquility. Honestly, I didn't know it was even possible; it was beyond my comprehension.

When Tsee opened her eyes, she realized I had gone rigid—I was frozen, immovable, with my mouth wide open. My wife immediately slapped me on my left cheek, and more than a little distressed, she said, "Salad, what happened to you?" I fell over onto the bed and snapped out of the trance.

"I don't know what happened, Tsee . . . I saw the bright light and felt this overwhelming love and peace, then I just froze." I stopped momentarily to process what had happened. Then, I spoke again. "Tsee, I could taste honey on my tongue, and then tears just started rolling out of my eyes." My wife smiled, then exhaled a deep sigh, which appeared to signify a mixture of relief and satisfaction.

"The Lord is inside of you, Salad," Tsee grinned. "You have received the Holy Spirit!"

"Really?" I was mystified. My godly wife nodded. Thankfully she had been preparing for this day in faith, so we prayed the prayer of repentance, holding hands and, on our knees, bowed reverently before Almighty God.

The bright, radiant light had not left; it still enveloped us, hovering like the Spirit of God brooding over the primeval waters of the deep. I felt something extremely powerful, but in my ignorance, it was indescribable. It was as though the Spirit of God had turned our room into a holy place. My heart beat with the weight and persistence of a powered hammer. The Holy Spirit had taken residence within my very being, and it was overwhelming. I was astonished that I had been frozen, perhaps by the shock of it all, but I could still taste honey on my tongue. That's when I started to sob. I cried and cried, deep and long. Tears of relief, joy, and gratitude streamed from my eyes. By the grace and power of God, He radically saved me.

What a rollercoaster ride the last twenty-four hours had been. I had experienced such terrible fear the previous evening, and now I was sitting in my room on that glorious Sunday morning, feeling bathed in pure love. I felt a deep calm settle within me. There were no thoughts demanding my attention. I was swimming in a deep blue lake of what Tsee said was my Heavenly Father's love.

Despite my extremely supernatural evening and morning, God wasn't done yet. I suddenly experienced a powerful vision of my new Lord, Jesus Christ. Standing before me, He wore a twisted crown of thorns pressed painfully into His head, causing rivulets of blood to stream down His face. I gasped at the sight, clutching my mouth. It convicted me of my sinful lifestyle. Tears filled my eyes again, and I began to weep, knowing He had been savagely tortured and murdered in my place. I had deserved such punishment, but He had spared me out of pure love. I dropped from the bed to the floor and started thanking Jesus for dying on the cross and for how much He loved me.

I had never experienced such profound love. My father died when I was three years old, and in Hmong culture, a widow can remarry soon after her husband's death, which my mother did. Another idiosyncrasy in our culture is that a widow may only take her daughters into her subsequent marriage. My mother had five sons and one daughter, which meant my four brothers and I were abandoned to fend for ourselves from an early age. I had never known what it was like to have a father, so I was thoroughly overwhelmed by this lavish outpouring of my Heavenly Father's pure adoration. In one life-changing moment, I was immersed in His love, grace, peace, and glory altogether. I was also instantly delivered from my longtime craving for hard liquor and beer. Arrogance and the prideful attitudes I had developed also dropped off me like shed snakeskin. All my worldly desires fell away instantly—my love of nightclubs, my desire for the admiration of worldly friends, and every carnal longing.

The next day I trashed all my household idols: all the pictures of Buddha, Ganesh, griffon images, and Pokémon toys, which I just knew had a demonic influence over them (Pokémon literally means "pocket monster"). I was completely free because when the Son sets you free, you are free indeed! (John 8:36). Unfortunately, although my heart had been made brand new, there were still sins of the past that would come back to haunt me.

On December 3, 2014, my wife and I woke suddenly at exactly 8:00 a.m. I immediately began to tell her about the dream I'd had just before waking. In the dream, we were seated at a great banquet table, surrounded by many guests. Many of the people were our friends or associates, some of whom we knew well. The table was laden with exotic foods, and many of the people were calling out for me, clamoring for my attention. One woman, our neighbor, was calling out explicit and unmentionable things.

It was a bizarre dream, and it left me feeling unnerved. When I had set the scene for Tsee, describing the table, she stared at me suspiciously . . . "I had this same dream, Salad!"

"What?" I was stunned by my wife's claim and unsure if she was serious. Tsee, however, began describing nearly the identical scene to the one in my dream, but what shocked me was when she started mentioning the names of the people seated at the table. A chill ran down my spine, and with wide eyes, I asked, "Tsee, how did you know? How did you know these people were in my dream?"

"I told you! I had the same dream, Salad," Then my wife's face grew cold and hard as she sat thinking about her dream. She spoke again. "I had the same dream, Salad, and it made me uncomfortable because I knew something was going on between you and our neighbor who was calling out your name. She was constantly calling out for you to do disgusting things."

My stomach sank.

"What are you hiding from me, Salad? You may think you can hide things from me, but you can't hide anything from God because He is the Father of all truth, and He knows everything we do."

I could only stare at my wife, who now glared at me with an expression that frightened me more than the demons had. "Salad..." Tsee demanded, her face like stone. "Have you been seeing this woman?"

"I... Tsee... I didn't mean to... I swear,"—I stuttered, unable to find the right words. I was suddenly fearful that all the love and joy I had experienced would be taken away. I was guilty as sin. And somehow, my wife had realized that through this dream we'd both had about my past. The weird thing was I had already turned my back on everything from that life the day before. I wanted nothing to do with that woman. I was disgusted with myself and couldn't believe what I had done in the past.

My thoughts were sharply interrupted by my wife's shrill, piercing shriek. I nearly jumped out of my skin. She jumped out of bed, her eyes crazy and wide. I emitted an involuntary, defensive grunt and recoiled back on the bed as she lunged forward, but she passed me and stormed out of the bedroom.

"Tsee! My love!" I called after her, springing out of bed and running to catch up to my wife. "Go back to your room!" I ordered, seeing Emily's shocked face pop out of her bedroom doorway. She quickly retreated as I followed Tsee into the kitchen.

As fast as I had run to catch up to my wife in the kitchen, I turned on my heel and dashed back the other way. Tsee marched toward me with a huge butcher's knife, her face twisted with rage. I had no idea what state of mind she was in, and for a second, it crossed my mind that maybe one of those demons had overtaken her. In a split-second decision, I ducked into Emily's room to protect the girls, just in case. "Get behind me!" I barked to the girls, who scurried behind me as I braced myself.

I was surprised yet again when Tsee stormed past the girl's room. So I edged forward and poked my head out of the doorway. I saw her walking into our room. What crossed my mind in that crazy moment almost made my heart stop: *She is going to kill herself in the bedroom.*

She didn't die, but what happened next made her wish she had.

***

I shifted position on the uncomfortable prison bench, leaned against the cold concrete wall, and stared up at the bright, fluorescent light, sighing. *My life is over.* I had never felt so betrayed, worthless, and hopeless. I didn't want to see a single person I knew ever again. The shame and betrayal made me feel dead—as if life had ended in hell.

When my husband confessed his unfaithfulness, sticky images of filth flooded my mind. They clung to my thoughts. *How could he be so sickeningly unfaithful without me knowing a thing? What else has he done behind my back?*

I thought back to my violent reaction. Sadness filled me, not because of my behavior in front of Salad but in front of the children. I was unable to keep my emotions in check. I had grabbed the biggest, sharpest knife we had and maniacally shredded every item of clothing in my husband's closet—his shirts, ties, suits . . . I purposed to rip his clothes to shreds, and then I would leave. I hoped to never again lay eyes on the man who had betrayed me in the most humiliating way.

Amid my rage, I wiped away a tear. For just a moment, I glimpsed my children's terrified eyes as I stormed past our bedroom. *I knew I would never hurt them, but they were terrified.* When Emily called the police, Salad nor I had any idea. Salad shouted that the police were there, which jolted me out of my rage, at least for the moment. I managed to keep up appearances and told the police everything was fine, so they left, but as soon as they did, my rage boiled over again—red hot, seething, uncontrollable. I grabbed the knife and started again.

Having given up any semblance of control, I ratcheted up the violence even more, terrifying my family further. I used the knife on shoes, pants, shorts, t-shirts, and even luggage. Anything and everything was fair game. I raged, ripping, shredding, screaming, and shrieking like a possessed woman.

The second time Emily called the police, they insisted on entering the premises. This time Emily quickly told them about the knife and the clothes. When the officers saw the closet, they promptly detained me and took me to jail—someplace I never thought I would go.

As I stared out the back window of the squad car, the cuffs cutting into my wrists, arms uncomfortably restrained behind my back, I swore I would never return! I shrugged off the distant whisper in my heart to forgive all those who had hurt me, just as God had forgiven me. I was unable to forgive Salad.

I had been scrupulously faithful to my husband, naively believing he had been faithful too. With tear-filled eyes again, I thought, *so many years of my life were wasted on a lie. I can't forgive him, and I can't forgive Emily, either.* They were both beyond redemption in my eyes, and I had made up my mind to leave them. *When I am released from jail, even though I know God hates divorce, I will leave.* I sat thinking about all the things my husband had been hiding from me to justify leaving. When the memory of my husband praying on his knees, the room awash with a golden glow, flickered across my mind, I pushed it away. I had been praying for my husband's redemption for years, but I had never suspected his path had been so bad.

Swamped by helplessness and a hollow sense of worthlessness, I was certain the Lord had left me. *How will God forgive me if I cannot forgive two of the most important people in my life? I am sure He cannot. I am already in hell. I am dead, and there is no way out.* Overwhelmed by anger again, not caring about anything, everything had lost meaning. I sat on the prison bench with my hands covering my face and elbows resting on my knees, knowing my life was ruined.

It was almost 6:00 p.m. when I finally cried out to God: "Oh Lord, I've wronged you so much. I'm unable to forgive my husband for his treachery, nor our daughter for calling the police." I sat momentarily, wondering if I should be truthful, then continued my prayer, "Lord, neither can I forgive that wicked woman who seduced my husband. I know I will never see You again. I am already in hell, serving the sentence I deserve. I know You are no longer with me." I wept at these awful emotions, wondering what would become of me. I had never felt so hopeless.

Suddenly I heard an audible voice. I knew that voice—it was the second time I had heard it. I sat up, releasing my face from my hands. The voice wasn't emanating from inside me. It was not coming through my ears nor from my heart —*it filled the whole room.*

It was the voice of the Lord! He had spoken! His words resonated through my being, from the top of my head to the soles of my feet. I wiped my eyes with the palms of my hands and took a deep breath. My heart burned like the midday sun. My Heavenly Father's voice spoke firmly but lovingly, "Tsee, I am with you. Do you not feel how hotly your heart burns within you? This is a sure sign I am still with you—my Spirit lives inside of you. I never left you. This is why you feel my burning hot fire inside your very being." The vibrant warmth emanated from my soul, and I knew it was my heavenly Father's radiant love welling up inside of me. I managed a little smile and stopped crying.

The Spirit of the Lord continued ministering life to me, saying, "You don't quite grasp it yet, but your husband is very ignorant of my ways. Due to his spiritual ignorance, this woman—for many years now—has been performing witchcraft on you and your family, and this is how your daughter became so sick. Tsee, it is not only this woman who has been practicing witchcraft against you. There are many people around you who have been casting malevolent spells on your family. It has been happening for many years now."

I wondered at these words. *Could it be?* It sure made a lot of sense, and it would explain the weird incident with the shadow at the karaoke machine and Salad seeing the demons. Anger began to surge within me at the thought of how Emily had suffered. Those demons had used these curses to infect her brain, causing multiple seizures, loss of memory, and loss of motor skills. Suddenly my anger and bitterness gave way to deep sorrow and compassion for my husband and daughter. Yes, my husband had committed these terrible sins, but he was lost—an atheist sinner dead to righteousness. I remembered the scripture from when I was saved—2 Corinthians 5:17 "Therefore, if anyone *is* in Christ, *he is* a new creation; old things have passed away; behold, all things have become new." *He is not the same man. That man died when Salad repented. Truly he is a new man, and God has revealed this so we can move past it.*

I dropped to my knees on the cold concrete floor and bowed my head, "Lord, please forgive me. I didn't know Emily's suffering and Salad's unfaithfulness were the results of witchcraft. I forgive my husband, Lord. I forgive Emily, and I even forgive that wicked woman. Lord, if you can save even her. Please forgive her." It took a lot for me to pray the last part, but I felt a spiritual release when I did—a burden lifted. I sat up on the iron bench and smiled.

Then, I felt a strong sense that this evil lady was aware of what was happening to my family, and worse yet, I *knew* the woman was using potent witchcraft to summon even more malevolent demons to attack my family. I had to alert my husband—he needed to pray. I didn't know how to use the phone in jail, so I asked a Caucasian woman who was sitting at a nearby table, and the woman showed me how to use the phone. Salad's number just rang and went to voicemail.

"You doing okay, honey?" the woman asked. She looked a little weathered from life, but her eyes were kind.

"I guess. . ." I sighed. "I wish I could speak to my husband."

The lady nodded and put a reassuring hand on my arm. "What happened, hun?"

I started telling the woman my story, outlining what had happened. The woman listened intently, and her face showed empathy, so I mentioned that God had just revealed that a particular woman had been practicing witchcraft against my family and me. The Caucasian lady's interest was piqued, so she asked for more detail. I ran my fingers through my hair as I described the woman.

"Whoa!" the Caucasian lady exclaimed. "I think I *know* this woman!"

I frowned, more than a little skeptical.

"Does she work at the holistic therapy center and is very involved with the Hmong community?"

I was stunned. "Yes! You actually know her?"

"I do!" The Caucasian woman nodded vigorously.

She began to tell me how she personally knew of several cases in which this wicked woman had been destroying the lives of people, breaking up marriages, and how some people had even died as a result of her witchcraft.

"Oh yeah. . . she is a real piece of work. I heard that she began messing with witchcraft, and then she got cancer, so she struck a deal with the devil that as long as she curses people and seduces them into messed up things, her cancer is kept away."

I felt like I was dreaming. It was all so surreal—there I was in the jail cell with this woman confirming what I had heard in my spirit. *How strange is this day?* I marveled. Armed with this new information, I started dialing my husband's number again, desperate to warn him of the danger he and the children were facing. At 6:00 p.m. exactly, I tried calling him repeatedly, but the phone just rang and rang. I thought of calling my parents or one of her siblings to alert them so they could pray and help, but I couldn't remember their phone numbers.

I thanked the lady for her help and excused myself back to the bench, where I started praying in earnest, especially because my husband didn't really know how to pray—he had only been saved for three days. On and on, I prayed, crying out before the Lord, not caring what the other inmates thought, until around midnight. I was exhausted. "Lord, I must get some sleep now. Please reveal the solution to this problem in a dream, Lord."

I lay on the bench, closed my eyes, and fell asleep instantly. Not long after, I started dreaming. My niece and I were standing outside my family home, praying. We couldn't go inside for some reason, but while we were praying, I saw a thick, dark cloud hovering over our house. Scary lightning bolts clapped through the night sky, and suddenly a violent thunderstorm began buffeting our house. In my dream, I prayed fervently against the lightning, but it didn't seem to be helping. Then I heard the voice of God boom out: "Why are you sleeping? Get up and pray!"

I was jolted awake and rubbed my eyes, looking around. A nearby inmate gave me a curious glance but then looked away. I started praying earnestly in tongues without ceasing until six in the morning. At that precise moment, I saw a vision. It was an open vision of three huge angels guarding our house. One was stationed on each side of the home, while the largest of the three angels stood sentry right in the middle, holding a giant sword. A glow of holiness filled the entire atmosphere around the home as the angels scrutinized the landscape for any sign of intruders. I breathed a sigh of relief because, at this point, I knew my family was safe.

At nine in the morning, a guard walked up to the cell and called out, "Tsee Vang!" I looked around nervously, believing I was in trouble, and asked another inmate what was happening. The woman

The Sword, the Serpent, and the Spiritual Realm

told me not to worry, it simply meant I had been released, and someone was there to take me home. My spirit lifted, and I wondered if my sister had heard I was in jail and had come to bail me out.

"Who has come to bail me out?" I asked the guard. He shrugged, implying he had no idea.

They guided me into an office to sign the release papers, and when I examined them, I saw Salad's name on the form. My heart pounded; my body trembled. Then the elevator doors opened, and I saw my husband standing there. Instantly, tears rolled down my cheeks. My cousin from Minnesota and my cousin's husband were standing with Salad. They had come to fetch me. I ran to Salad and hugged him tightly, crying tears of joy. I started to ask him to forgive me, but before I could utter the words, Salad cried, "Please forgive me, my precious wife! I was lost and stupid. That man is gone. I will never hurt you again!" I fell into his arms, and we wept together.

"Of course, my husband. Please forgive me too. I will never behave like that again."

Salad put his hands on my shoulders and smiled. I smiled back; my eyebrows creased in a frown, "We're going to have to go shopping to get you some new clothes, Salad. . ." He threw back his head in laughter and hugged me tighter.

"Let's get out of here," he said. "What a strange few days, huh? You'll never believe what we went through last night."

"Oh, I think I know!" I looked up at him. "Wait until I tell you what one of the other inmates told me!"

"Therefore if anyone is in Christ [that is, grafted in, joined to Him by faith in Him as Savior], he is a new creature [reborn and renewed by the Holy Spirit]; the old things [the previous moral and spiritual condition] have passed away. Behold, new

things have come [because spiritual awakening brings a new life]. But all these things are from God, who reconciled us to Himself through Christ [making us acceptable to Him] and gave us the ministry of reconciliation [so that by our example we might bring others to Him], that is, that God was in Christ reconciling the world to Himself, not counting people's sins against them [but canceling them]. And He has committed to us the message of reconciliation [that is, restoration to favor with God]." (2 Corinthians 5:17-19 AMP)

Under the Old Covenant, even great prophets like Moses had limited access to God's Spirit. However, as a fulfillment of the New Covenant, the Holy Spirit dwells in the hearts of believers, and they are continually conformed to the image of Jesus Christ. That happens through understanding God's revelation hidden in Christ, Himself. In Him dwells the fullness of God. He is the very image of God. Through faith, the Holy Spirit enables the believer to experience a new way of life that resembles Christ and reflects His glory.

CHAPTER 5: HOME INVASION

I gently touched my wife's arm, asking if she needed anything to eat or drink. I was ready to cook her a five-course meal, but she only asked for some cold water, which I quickly poured for her then we sat down together in the living room. I had to pry the children's arms from around their mother so she could have some space; they were so relieved she was home. I also felt a strong urge to hug her and reassure her I was a new man and would never dream of hurting her again. Something, however, told me she already knew that. Tsee had also changed—something I certainly hadn't expected. She was more compliant—not necessarily just to me—she'd always been respectful, but it was as though God had touched her. I knew something powerful had happened in that jail cell. My mind reeled as I pondered the previous two days. . . I'd gone from being a proud atheist to seeing demons, having spiritual dreams, and hearing a demonic war raging over my house throughout the night. If it were only me experiencing these things, I would have checked myself into a mental wellness facility.

"Are you okay, Tsee?" I smiled at my wife. She nodded and smiled back; it felt like Heaven was shining upon me for a second. I was so relieved to have my family. "What happened in jail? You seem. . . different—at peace." Tsee inhaled deeply, shaking her head. Then, she began to tell me about the night's events from her perspective. The children and I had experienced a spiritual war at the house, and it appeared Tsee had, too.

When she had finished recounting her evening's events, I was stunned. It was no wonder she looked tired—she had been praying all night, and I realized that she, too, had been fighting a spiritual war for our family. I saw Tsee through new eyes, recognizing her strength as a spiritual warrior—without her fervent prayers, I'm not sure the children and I would have survived the previous evening. Without her many months of enduring persecution from me—her own husband—I knew I would have been lost forever, waiting until it was too late before I became aware of those horrific monsters. I was also awestruck at our Heavenly Father's intervention. He had undoubtedly placed Tsee in the same cell as that Caucasian woman who knew this witch and the warlocks who were hell-bent on our destruction.

I asked Tsee how the Caucasian woman knew the witch who had seduced me. Tsee said the Caucasian woman knew about her through people who worked for the witch and the warlocks. They ran a business, and she knew some people who had worked with them—she had heard a few scary stories. Some people had even died through their witchcraft.

This supernatural manifestation was new to us—especially me, but how else does one explain all these occurrences? First, Tsee and I experienced the same dream. Next, the Caucasian woman was in the same cell as Tsee. Then, Tsee and I had related frightening spiritual experiences between midnight and 6:00 a.m. while in separate physical locations.

Tsee commented that I looked like I hadn't slept much either, and I smiled weakly. I then began to tell her the story of our crazy evening. The police took Tsee to jail around 9:00 the prior morning. Shortly after she left, I started hearing unearthly whispers in the house that sent shivers down my spine. I was terrified the same monsters I had seen at the bar two nights before would walk through the walls of my house. Next, I heard them very clearly on the phone. Warbling, growling voices mixed in with a scratchy static hiss were so bad I couldn't even place a phone call. It was like something out of a horror movie. When darkness fell, things cranked up a notch. The children

The Sword, the Serpent, and the Spiritual Realm

and I heard crashing and clanging on the house's roof. It sounded like a battle of clashing swords raging and ringing through the night air. Shivering, I peeked through the blinds, but no wind disturbed the trees, and the neighbors seemed unfazed. By all other accounts, the evening was calm, with no visible disturbances. The children, however, were as freaked out as I was. I started praying the only thing I knew to say: I asked Jesus for protection. I frantically muttered these prayers over a cup of water, which I then took and sprinkled on every window and doorway. I didn't know if it would work, but I figured my homemade batch of "holy water" wouldn't hurt.

When the eerie cacophony of battle swords escalated, I gathered all six children together to sleep in the living room. I was too terrified to sleep, so I sat on the couch and did the only thing I knew to give us some protection—I sang a song in my native Hmong tongue: "Tswv Yexus Lub Npe Zoo Kawg Nkaus," which, when translated into English means, "The Lord Jesus' Name is Perfect."

As I sang, I thought about my wife's rage. It seemed as if a demon of violence had temporarily possessed her—she was uncontrollable. Sadness and guilt descended over me. I knew I had opened the door to this attack on my family and didn't know how to stop it. Things seemed okay when Tsee and I prayed together, but now everything had fallen apart. I had done so much wrong. I had been so focused on myself, and now my wife was in jail because of it. I saw clearly how these malevolent spirits caused us all to feel such powerful emotions—lust, fear, rage. . . but it was terrifying. They could manifest themselves in the physical realm.

While I pondered all of this, the phone rang multiple times. It was Tsee. Despite my despair, the devil's voice would whisper, "Don't answer. She's going to manipulate you. She wants you to bring her back home so she can kill you." Not realizing that subtle whisper was the devil, I was too afraid to answer.

With the continuing noise above our house, I decided to peek through the blinds again and quickly wished I hadn't. This time, I could hear the spiritual world and see demons and angels as clearly as I saw my children huddled together in the living room. They were genuinely horrifying.

I was about to run back to the children when I realized a host of heavenly angels were warring against the demons. I saw giant celestial beings shimmering in golden light, swooping down and striking the monsters. I realized the noise above our house was angels taking the fight to the demons. It was all mesmerizing, but I was still terrified. I wanted to believe we were protected, but the demonic horde appeared to outnumber the angelic host. Then, after seeing the angels, I had a thought. I ran across the house and looked out the window, and saw angels had taken up positions on that side of the house, too, and realized they had formed a rectangle around our house, positioning heavenly sentries on each of the four sides. Then, since my eyes were opened, I saw it . . . one huge angel was standing guard right in the middle of our living room where we had gathered.

I dropped the gap in the blinds through which I was peeking and shut my eyes tightly before opening them to see if the angel was still there. He was, so I crept back to the huddle of children, climbed under the blanket, and gathered them around me.

The children slept fitfully from about 9:00 p.m., but when I could hear the battle getting worse, I would wake them occasionally to help me sing the one song of protection I knew. At 2:00 a.m., the fight became almost unbearable. I trembled under the covers as what sounded like hundreds, if not thousands, of demons shrieking, growling, and screaming as they attempted to enter the house with what I could only assume was a vicious bloodlust. For an hour, this portion of the battle raged, and then it slowly decreased in intensity. I sang that Hmong song until it was burned into my memory. The angel stood with us all night, strong, silent, and watchful.

The children slept as I mostly stared at them, singing softly while the battle raged. That continued from 3:00 a.m. to 4:00 a.m., then to 5:00 a.m., and then suddenly, at 6:00 a.m.—it stopped. My head perked up, and I listened closely . . . Nothing—not even a little snarl or the lone crash of swords. I looked over at the spot where the angel had been standing, and if he was still there, I could no longer see him. I jumped up, still a little nervous, but somehow I knew God had won.

As tired as she was, Tsee's eyes were wide with awe as I finished my account of the evening. We had won the victory with God's help, but that was the most harrowing, scary night of my life. I realized it was probably even more difficult for Tsee because, from her jail cell, she had seen a vision of the demons and knew they were gathering at our home to attack our family. What fascinated me was God's timing; after praying all night fervently, right when Tsee felt the release in her spirit at 6:00 a.m., she saw an open vision of three large angels. One of them held a giant sword while they all guarded our house. She knew it was over. She sensed it in her spirit.

I got up, walked over to my wife, and hugged her tightly. I was so grateful for her; I knew God had allowed us to see and recognize these dark forces for a reason. Despite being separated by location, we'd fought together, and God had brought us out of the darkness into His marvelous light, revealing His power and glory. I was so happy had not lost my family, even if it took the scariest night I had experienced to that point. That is how we truly came to God and placed Him first in our marriage. And it was just the beginning of supernatural things God would do through us. That same day, we would have yet another significant supernatural experience.

Vision of the World
After that night, I immediately lost all taste for anything carnal. My family has a generational custom—it is widespread for men to marry two or three wives, sometimes even four. After the horror of what I had experienced and God's miraculous intervention, He had

thoroughly broken that spirit of polygamy. When the Holy Spirit entered my being, I no longer had the slightest interest in this idea. This cleansing happened to the point that the same day, I went through the house and threw out anything that I knew wasn't godly; all the Pokémon toys, the griffon images I had, secular music, traditional Hmong amulets and trinkets—everything. I kept digging out more and more items that might bind me to my old life. I poured out all my liquor, smashed every household idol, and threw out anything that connected to my old life.

The same morning a niece from Minnesota heard my account of the evening and then heard Tsee's account, and she had a suggestion. She said she could arrange for a Hmong prophet from Minnesota to visit us. She said his name was Mr. Peter Yang, and he may know how to help us keep these demons at bay permanently. We were overjoyed when my niece said Mr. Yang felt led to come immediately, and he could be there that evening.

While waiting for him to arrive, Tsee and I decided to spend some time in prayer in the living room. To be honest, even though God had done a miraculous work, I was pretty traumatized, even asking Tsee to go to the bathroom with me in case the demons appeared again. Tsee and I had been praying for a little while when suddenly, the presence of God became immensely strong in the room. We both felt weak and fell to the ground in reverential fear of the Lord. As we did, instantly, our eyes were mutually opened to the supernatural yet again.

Suddenly Tsee's hair became radiantly white. Her garments also shone a brilliant white, and her skin radiated a glowing purity. I was shocked at her appearance, but more so that she appeared startled at mine. I looked down at my clothes, shining the most brilliant white I'd ever seen. Apparently, my face and hair were shining too. Then, appearing like a giant hologram in front of us, an open vision unfolded of two gleaming candles growing closer and closer together. Then the two merged and became one big, very bright candle.

Next, we saw a globe of the entire world directly in front of us, and on the map of the Earth, many countries shone and twinkled like stars. The vision lingered for several moments, then quickly dissipated. Tsee and I were stunned at the vision and worshiped the Lord in awe of what we'd just seen. We were unsure what the vision meant, but we realized that Prophet Peter Yang's visit was very likely in God's timing.

We told Prophet Yang about the vision when he arrived later that evening. We had never met the man before, but when he started to speak, we both instantly knew he was a true prophet of God. He talked to me directly, but he confirmed, just as the vision showed, that we are one flame in the sight of God. The prophet told me when God chooses a person to perform a specific task for His Kingdom, Satan will use every force available to prevent the person's success. He said this is why all these strange occurrences were happening in our lives and that the devil had been working hard to lure us away, to distract us from God's presence.

He said I would be like the apostle Paul, going from place to place, the first among the Hmong people to witness to the world. He said the Hmong people, who had never seen God's power before—both believers and non-believers—would see the demonstration of God's power, and He would open their eyes. The prophet told us signs would open up the believers' spiritual eyes and cause the non-believers to come to the Lord, especially after seeing firsthand our God is the one true God of the universe. He said many idol worshipers would turn to God.

"Your ministry will start here in Appleton," he proclaimed, "and from here, it will burst out to all the nations." "Have you heard of Billy Graham?" he asked me next.

"No," I replied. "Who's that?"

"He's a well-known evangelist, Salad, and soon you will not only lay hands on people, but the words you speak out of your mouth will enable thousands to be healed." He continued, "God anointed you with the gift of healing and miracles. Six months from now, you will lay hands on the sick, and they will be healed."

I was shocked and slightly overwhelmed, so I asked him, "What does that mean?"

He continued, saying only, "In your lifetime, you will see many dead people raised from the dead, and you will be the first Hmong international evangelist to travel all over the world, preaching before thousands of people. Furthermore, in three years, you will be a pastor." He then said I would leave a legacy, telling me, "Even after you are no longer here on Earth, people will still remember how God has used you for His Kingdom." Finally, the prophet of God said, "At this point in your life, you keep calling me older brother, but one day, it will be the other way around— I will be looking up to you as an older brother."

I raised my hands to the Lord, wept, and worshiped. The presence of God was so thick I felt like I could swim in it. But I was still a baby Christian. Just the night before, I had seen horrific demons, so after a few minutes, I asked Prophet Yang if he and the friend who came with him might stay in our guest room that night. Prophet Yang smiled and agreed.

"And this gospel of the kingdom will be preached in the whole world as a testimony to all nations, and then the end will come." (Matthew 24:14 NIV

And He said to them, "Go into all the world and preach the gospel to every creature. He who believes and is baptized will be saved; but he who does not believe will be condemned. And these signs will follow those who believe: In My name they will cast out demons; they will speak with new tongues; they will take up serpents;

and if they drink anything deadly, it will by no means hurt them; they will lay hands on the sick, and they will recover." (Mark 16:15-18 NKJV)

Christ commissioned His followers to represent His kingdom here on Earth and share the Good News with all men. He gives believers the keys to the Kingdom of Heaven. Whatever we bind on Earth will be bound in heaven, and whatever we loose on Earth will be loosed in heaven (Matthew 16:19). These keys are authorization given to us by the Word of God. Therefore, authority follows ministers of the Word when they exercise these keys. Jesus, the Great Commissioner, has approved his ministers to open (to loose) and shut (to bind). It is the highest honor He could bestow—to be God's representative to declare the Gospel to the world, to herald its salvation, which is the reunion between God and men.

CHAPTER 6: DREAM TRAINING

"Can I pray for you?" I asked. We had tried everything else, including medicine, nutrition counseling, exercise, and chiropractic treatments, but it was not working.

"Yeah, sure—anything that helps," he winced through the discomfort, having come into the clinic bent over in severe back pain.

"They always say that—'Anything that helps,'" I thought and continued.

"Okay, in Mark 16:18, the Bible says, lay hands on the sick, and they shall be healed. Can I put my hand on your back?"

"Yes, go ahead."

In his willingness, he didn't know that I had already prayed for 100 people in my clinic—and they *didn't* get healed—not one of them. He was patient 101, and I was not discouraged. I remembered Prophet Yang's words, and they gave me faith. Throughout the previous 100 patient visits, God was teaching me about healing, deliverance, and the power of Jesus' name. He was building my faith, and something different happened when I prayed for this man—the 101st Christian to come into the clinic after I reopened it.

"I feel something warm coming out of my stomach into my hand. Do you feel something warm in your back too?" I asked in slight surprise.

"Yeah, I feel something warm in my back too."

"I don't know what it is, but I think it's God helping you and healing you. So I'm going to take my hands off now, okay?"

"Okay."

By the time my hand left his back, he was standing up straight in my office.

"How do you feel? Is there any more pain?"

"I'm pain-free," he managed to utter with amazement.

We both scratched our heads at what had just happened. "This is crazy!" I thought to myself. Is this what Prophet Yang was talking about when he said, "Salad, . . . soon you will not only lay hands on people, but the words you speak out of your mouth will enable thousands to be healed. God anointed you with the gift of healing and miracles. Six months from now, you will lay hands on the sick, and they will be healed." Yes! My faith was ignited!

From that day, after praying for patient 101, it felt like fire or heat was always coming out of my left hand and the left side of my body. I started to see little healings and miracles when I laid hands on people—little, itsy bitsy healings and miracles if there's such a thing. Later, people were healed from "big things" like cancer and incurable diseases when I laid my hands on them. But in the beginning—the first few to six months after patient 101—it was little minor stuff like soreness, back pain, neck pain, etc.

I call it "little minor stuff," but it was a breakthrough in my spiritual development. God had been working through dreams to get me to that day—dreams that He had used like a training ground to build my faith.

The Sword, the Serpent, and the Spiritual Realm

***

"In Jesus' name, disappear!" I declared in the dream. Bam! Without hesitation, the demon lay down flat on the ground.

The demon was about two or three feet tall and looked like an alien with a big head and big eyes. Like E.T. trying to phone home, it resembled those Unidentified Flying Objects (UFO) aliens with short legs and arms. At first, I thought, "Oh, it's a UFO. It's not a demon; it's a UFO or an extra-terrestrial being from space." But God was helping me work through my fear of demons by letting me first see them as alien beings, and I realized Jesus's name had power over them.

This was just the beginning of a series of dreams that began around the time of Prophet Yang's visit in December 2014. They intensified from the time of his visit and the clinic closing to when I reopened the clinic in February 2015. Before his visit, fear had gripped me. Remember, I had asked Tsee to accompany me to the bathroom and Prophet Yang and his friend to stay overnight in our guest room because I feared the horrific demons I had seen. But through each dream, God uprooted fear from my life and built my faith.

For example, I was severely afraid of snakes. And in later dreams, I would confront seven-foot green snakes, then fifteen-foot, and next, a thirty-foot dragon as wide as a cow, coming out of a river where I was standing on top of a bridge to attack me.

Amidst all the dreams and transformations in my life, I had less desire to do secular work at the clinic. Then, one day, while looking at the certificates and diplomas on my office walls, I realized they had become idols to me, things I had exalted higher than the knowledge of God. They were symbols of the pride of life, and I didn't want that worldly mindset anymore; I had surrendered to God. "For all that is in the world, the lust of the flesh, and the lust of the eyes, and the pride of life, is not of the Father, but is of the world" (1 John 2:16).

Also, I knew the diplomas couldn't help me with what I was seeing in my dreams and experiencing supernaturally through spiritual attacks. And after Prophet Yang's visit, in addition to all the dreams, we were bombarded with witchcraft attacks. I was trying to figure out all the supernatural encounters we were having while God was simultaneously transforming my heart. So I closed the clinic during the same month as Prophet Yang's visit. I later reopened it, but I wanted to serve God with all my heart. At the time, I didn't know that praying for people at the clinic would be part of my training. Everything was so intense, the dreams, the attacks—everything. So in the same way that I was choosing between a secular and ministry vocation, I was also making choices in my dreams.

One night, God showed me a vision of a dark, haunting, diverging road in a dream. On its right side was a hill where some people were holding lightbulbs. Subconsciously, I immediately knew there was nothing to fear on that side, but on the left, the road diverged into the woods and up an opposite hill. Like ghosts or demon spirits moving through their leaves, an evil wind was blowing through the trees on that side of the road. Then, in the dream, it was as if God told me which side of the road I should choose to test my faith and overcome the demons. But I had a choice between the right side, where the lights were, and the left side, where the dark winds and demons were.

I kept walking, approaching the division in the road, and still deciding what I would do. The people holding the lights were inviting, and there was no fear on that side of the road. But when I considered the left side, I was frightened. So that night, in the dream, I chose the right side of the road. But it wasn't over. I had the same dream again the next night and would have to confront my fears again.

The second night, in the dream, I went to the left side of the road to test my faith against fear and evil spirits. I got halfway to the lower part of the hill and stopped. Then I woke up in fear. Still, it wasn't over. I had the same dream a third time the next night. God gave me another chance to confront my fears.

The Sword, the Serpent, and the Spiritual Realm

The third night, I went to the left side again toward the trees and hill. This time, the wind confronted me with high-pitched howling, wooing, and whooshing. With sounds I had never heard, the winds pressed against me, attempting to imprint fear in my soul. But I said to myself, "I must go. I am not afraid. I can do it with God. I can do it." Then I went through the valley of the hill, and after that, I had courage in my dream. I moved past the lower part of the hill to the top.

I was conquering fear with faith; then, it happened. Thousands of dark, black, twelve-foot twisters were coming at me in every direction—as if tornadoes were trying to pierce my soul. But like a superhero with my own force field, they did not hit me. As I moved against the winds, the twisters either missed me or I walked right through them. I knew I had overcome fear by the time I got to the top of the hill. I was no longer afraid; I had gone through the valley and didn't even care that the twisters were coming at me. After three nights of fierce training, I had reached the hilltop and exercised strong faith. God was teaching me how to deal with fear and demons.

For God hath not given us the spirit of fear; but of power, and of love, and of a sound mind. (2 Timothy 1:7 KJV)

Next, in a single dream, God exposed the seducing spirit of adultery.

She was a brunette no taller than the height from the floor to my eyebrows. She stood at my right side as a man talked during the meeting. Then she turned, went around my back, and reached out to hold me from behind. I knew she was trying to seduce me into adultery. She didn't have to say a word; her actions were as clear as the day's sunlight, and God made it clear to me that what she was trying to do was wrong. I didn't have to say that, either. I knew it was wrong, and she knew that I knew.

The moment I said to myself that it was wrong, her flesh tore open as if a surgeon's knife had split her body into two halves—straight down the middle. A white spirit with crystal white, shining, glowing hair stepped out of her divided flesh—like a person who had lived inside a person. Its face was shining white. I threw rocks at it, as the two halves of the body fell to the ground, but it ran away up the hill. It was gone, the dream was finished, and that evil spirit had been exposed.

After that, I did not have any more dreams of women coming to seduce me or tempt me with sexual sins. I passed the test because I realized that it was wrong, and the evil spirit knew I did. I don't know how it knew, but it knew that I knew. And it got scared, came out of her body, and up and ran. The demon was exposed, and I had the victory.

For by means of a whorish woman a man is brought to a piece of bread: and the adultress will hunt for the precious life. (Proverbs 6:26 KJV)

After that, my dream training continued through another series of three dreams featuring muscular demons like the monsters in the Lord of the Rings movie.

They were like zombies from The Walking Dead. They tried to scare me with their bloody eyes, and when they approached, I punched them. Smack! I swung with all the strength I had. But unlike the UFO-looking demons in a previous dream, they did not fall down—they were stronger. So I kept punching them, blow after blow. Unfortunately, nothing I did worked, and the dream ended.

I had the same dream the next night for the second time. However, this time, God gave me knowledge and wisdom in my heart to use the name of Jesus. "In Jesus' name, be destroyed," I exclaimed in the dream, and they fell down, trembled, and disappeared. I knew that God was teaching me how to use Jesus' name. That worked on the zombie-like demons, but there was another giant, muscular demon about twenty or thirty feet tall. Nothing I did worked with him, not even Jesus' name. This wasn't a "worker" demon; it was a strongman.

The third night, I had the same dream, but to the muscle-bound, strong demon, I said, "Do you know who my Father is? My Father . . . He is the righteous judge. Are you afraid of Him?" The strongman shook like a leaf. God had given me the words to confront that muscle-bound demon on the third night. So every dream was like a training match—I was in the ring throwing punches at demons, and God was my boxing coach, teaching me how to do spiritual warfare. He taught me that He is the righteous judge and that demons are afraid of Him and His judgment. I only had to speak of the righteous judge; neither demons nor the strongman ever spoke back. They shook and disappeared.

But there is only one who is lawgiver and judge—the one who is able to save and destroy. (James 4:12a NET)

You believe that God is one; well and good. Even the demons believe that—and tremble with fear. (James 2:19 NET)

I was advancing in my training, passing the tests in my dreams, and my faith was growing quickly. I had all these dreams within a month. Then, on the night of January 14, 2015, God's voice came into the room.

Tsee was asleep, and I was worshipping and singing to the Lord in our bedroom. It was amazing because I had not been saved that long, but I thirsted for His presence. I continued singing until I was no longer the only one singing in the room. Though Tsee had been sleeping, she also heard it. God's voice began singing in our room, saying, "I've always been here. I will reveal myself to whoever I please to reveal." He was letting us know that He chooses some people to show things that He doesn't show to other people—now and in the future. And He does this to bring people from darkness to His saving light. He's going to choose whoever He desires and use them to work for His Kingdom. He will reveal things to them so that they can be a testimony to the world. He had chosen Tsee and me.

Then again, on February 3, 2015, we heard the voice of the Lord that night. It was like God woke us up in the middle of the night, speaking to us in an audible voice, saying, "I will not leave you. Be still; be patient. You're going through a learning process. I've always been here, don't be afraid." It was weird and new to us, but His voice was spiritually audible. It was like we could hear Him, but nobody else could. The presence of the Lord was undeniably in our room again, and we knew that He loved us. It was grace. It was about His love.

With all the dreams and visions of demons and angels, these were just the words we needed to hear—". . . don't be afraid." His voice was confirmation that we would need for the roller coaster called "church planting" that was ahead of us.

***

"Okay, does anybody need healing? A miracle?" I asked after coming to the stage uninvited. The senior pastor glared at me. "What are you doing?" he said with his eyes. The revival's guest preacher also looked at me disdainfully, but I had to do something. What he had just preached was carnal, and unable to help anyone in the service.

"Who's sick? Come up here." I declared. Some people began to move forward, but looking at me and then the two pastors for approval, they too were wondering what I was doing and if I was supposed to be on stage. Then, suddenly, a woman came to the front with back and neck pain, and she got healed.

"Anybody else?" I asked, and the people kept coming. One after the other, they were coming to the stage and getting healed. Healed! Healed! Then the two pastors decided not to look anymore. They were behind me, talking to people and pretending they didn't care. But did they ever!

After the service, they lectured me. They really let me have it. I didn't know that was only the beginning of the persecution I would face for bringing God's healing power to his people. Like Joseph in the Bible, my dream training was necessary, but not everyone would be happy with my dreams. Still, what those two pastors meant for evil, God would eventually use for my good. Their lecture and disdain were the beginning of the next phase of my training and church-planting education.

And when they saw him [Joseph] afar off, even before he came near unto them, they conspired against him to slay him. ⁱ⁹ And they said one to another, Behold, this dreamer cometh. ²⁰ Come now therefore, and let us slay him, and cast him into some pit, and we will say, Some evil beast hath devoured him: and we shall see what will become of his dreams. (Genesis 37:18-20 KJV, brackets added)

But as for you, ye thought evil against me [Joseph speaking about his brother's conspiracy]; but God meant it unto good, to bring to pass, as it is this day, to save much people alive. (Genesis 50:20 KJV, brackets added)

He sent a man before them, even Joseph, who was sold for a servant: ¹⁸ Whose feet they hurt with fetters: he was laid in iron: ¹⁹ Until the time that his word came: the word of the Lord tried him. (Psalm 105:17-19 KJV)

Joseph also went through dream training. Just as God told Tsee and me, He chose to show Joseph things that He didn't show other people, specifically Joseph's brothers, and they hated him for it. God gave Joseph a series of dreams, and after that, he went through a series of tests. He remained faithful, and God used him to save a nation and bring healing to his family. If you remain faithful during your training process and tests, God will also use you.

Salad Vang

CHAPTER 7: MORE MIRACLES, MORE PERSECUTION

"Hi Tsee, this is Eve. Do you remember me? You used to come to my husband's church years ago—Pastor Cai's church. Remember? I saw you and your husband in the park praying for people. How are you?"

"Oh yes. Hi, Eve. I'm well. What a surprise. You're married to Pastor Cai now? How are you?"

"Yeah, we're married now, and I'm good, thanks. It was so powerful—what I saw you and your husband doing in the park."

"Yes, my husband and I have been doing outreach and praying for people in different places. God told us we needed to start a fire for Him—to do something in the community to bring people to God."

"That's awesome. I'd love for your husband to meet my husband. Let's get together."

"Sure, we'd love to."

Eve was a spirit-filled believer and had recently married Pastor Cai, a Hmong Baptist pastor who had been widowed. She believed in healing, so she was so excited to see what we were doing in the park. But the park was just one of many outreaches we had been doing in public places. For example, once, during a public festival, we put up a tent with a sign in Hmong and English labeled

"Free Healing." The event was unforgettable, and full of unexpected consequences.

***

"In Jesus' name, come out of her," I commanded the demon, but it wasn't a dream this time. Instead, we were in the middle of a secular festival in Green Bay.

"Aiiiiiiiiiiieeeeeeeeeeeeeeeeee!" she shrilled. Only it wasn't her. It was the demon leaving her body with a scream so disturbing it shook our tent.

"Oh . . . oh my God. I'm healed," she said as if she had come back to herself. "Thank you. Thank you for praying for me."

"You're welcome. But do you know that Jesus is your healer? We are here so people can know that Jesus is real. He is the one who healed you, and He died to save you. Believe in Him, and you will be saved."

Like bees swarming, that festival was full of people like her. Some were passing by while others were moving in and out of our tent, including a celebrity from Laos, community leaders who were getting drunk with beer, and women and children eating and buying candy. Thousands of people were there.

Some onlookers in the crowd laughed as we prayed. Others used their cell phones to videotape us. We didn't care because people were getting healing and hearing about Jesus.

The drunken community leaders came to the tent as a group demanding to see me, but others discouraged them, telling them I didn't have time to see them. We had been busy praying for people all day, and unlike the 100 patients I had prayed for in my clinic, everyone we prayed for in that tent got healed—everyone one of them. The pain in their bodies left, blurry vision was healed, and blind eyes opened. So there was a lot of excitement being generated throughout the festival. It was a revival.

Many came into our tent as unbelievers, but when they got healed, they believed in Jesus and left out saved. They would leave the tent and tell other unbelievers at the festival to come because they got healed—and the people did come. Some were healed, others were delivered from demonic oppression, and many were saved. It was glorious, and we later learned that even the skeptic's videos went viral.

The day was packed with wonderful testimonies—but it wasn't without persecution. Although going viral on social media was like free advertisement for the Gospel, it also brought rebukes. Believers and unbelievers alike were saying that miracles were not real and that we were fake. But even through that, people came to know Jesus—and that's what really mattered.

The young and elderly, from five years old to those who were grandmas and grandpas, were watching what happened via YouTube. Although they ridiculed us, their videos became a documentation of God's healing power—for all to see. Many unbelievers learned about us through videos that we intended to mock us.

The Hmong people are from Laos and had never seen healing and miracles like that before, and the mockers' videos helped spread the truth to a people group that had never experienced it. That was a primary reason we did outreach—about 90% of the Hmong people did not believe in God. They believed in Shamanism and the demons of this world. Like the native Indians, they called the demons spirits. They would cover their faces and dance for the spirits, which is idol worship. They would not come into churches, so we went to festivals, parks, and other community events to bring unbelievers to God, and publicly declare that Jesus was alive and still healed. That day they came to our tent, and despite the ridicule, once again, what the devil meant for evil, God used for good to save many.

So when Eve, Pastor Cai's new wife, saw us in the park, we had already seen God heal so many people and were passionate to see more people experience Jesus and His miracles. She wanted us to meet her husband, and after a short while of getting to know them and knowing even less about the Baptist denomination, we zealously asked him about starting a church.

"Hey, Pastor, what do you think? Is it a good idea to start a church that's filled with the Holy Spirit, healing, miracles, and helping people?" I asked. He dismissed the idea at first, and I wasn't sure why. I didn't understand his reluctance. Still, Tsee and I started praying with him and his wife, and after a while, he decided that we should go ahead and open a church. He introduced us to another Baptist couple that he thought would be a good part of the church-planting team, and the three of us (three couples) opened a church in February 2015.

As we worked together and Tsee and I prayed for people who came, the church grew. Little by little, people were becoming members. Then, we had a revival and gave away free rice to anyone who wanted it. People came from everyone for free rice, and we invited a Baptist preacher to preach during the revival.

Sadly, his message was very carnal and worldly. He joked about going to Laos to get a second wife. He said he was just kidding, but it was inappropriate, and did nothing to help the people who had come. On the contrary, it encouraged ungodliness and immorality. On top of that, at the end of his sermon, there was no prayer—no healing—no miracles. I had had enough, and that's when I went to the stage and said, "Okay, does anybody need healing? A miracle?"

I went to the pulpit uninvited and asked anyone who was sick to come up for prayer. The senior pastor and guest preacher were irritated by my actions. But despite their lack of agreement, God healed many people, and they sang, "More miracles, more miracles."

The Sword, the Serpent, and the Spiritual Realm

After the service, the senior pastor and guest preacher gave me a lecture and expressed their disdain for how I had prayed for the sick. Instead of rejoicing for the healings that had happened, they were angered by them. My response was, "Well, Jesus did it. Those people came here sick, and they needed deliverance and healing." To my surprise, they responded, "We don't do that in our church." I think they thought that meant I would stop, but I didn't. However, I did have a realization.

From that day on, Tsee and I realized that people can be pastors or church members but not believe what the Bible teaches. We started to research and discovered that there were various denominations, and they believed different things about the Bible. We were operating out of the revelation from the genuine encounters we had experienced with demons and angels in our home and the knowledge of His love through His audible voice and visitations. We were zealous but did not know about denominations or that each denomination had different beliefs.

We realized that some denominations teach about speaking tongues, healings, and miracles, but others don't. We even visited a church and later learned that they had homosexual leadership and endorsed gay marriage—we got out of there quickly, but we were shocked by these rude awakenings. Still, we needed to be armed with that knowledge so we could grow because another big realization was on the way.

In September 2015, the district director of the Baptist churches came from Minnesota because he had heard about the healings that were taking place, and like us, he believed in miracles. He had a YouTube channel and wanted to videotape us praying for people. When the director came, the pastor, who had been a guest preacher during the "Free Rice" revival, approached him. He tried to convince the director to tell Tsee and me to stop praying for healing, casting out devils, and speaking in tongues. He said they didn't believe in demons—there were no demons, and if we didn't stop what we were doing, they would do something to us. Well . . . they did.

***

"He photoshopped the picture," the church treasurer told the members. "The things Brother Salad does are a lie."

"What is he doing?" I thought. "I prayed for him and his family, and they were all healed. Why is he doing this?"

"He's a fake! There was no miracle. The X-rays were photoshopped. Don't believe him," he insisted.

You could see dread on the faces of some congregation members and fear and confusion in others as he spoke. Then, the whispering started, and standing there in front of the church listening to him, I was livid.

A woman had brought her son into the clinic. He suffered from scoliosis, so I asked his mother if I could pray for him and take an X-ray afterward? She agreed. So I x-rayed him after praying, and his spine was straight. Then I brought the X-ray to the church as a testimony and showed them the miracle for God's glory. It was a miracle healing.

But now, in front of the whole church, this brother was saying I was a fake—someone I had prayed for and who personally had been healed. I couldn't understand it. I cycled through anger, confusion, and grief then, back to anger. How could he, the treasurer of a church I helped establish, do this? Why would he do this?

My emotions were out of control not only because of that brother's betrayal but also because I had invested so much in the church—prayers, money, time, and more. I had done the church's registration and legal paperwork, opened its bank account, prayed for people . . . "How could this be happening," I thought. "Is he after money? They can have it—the money in the account—anything they want. But I'm not coming to this church anymore."

The Sword, the Serpent, and the Spiritual Realm

I was done. I went outside and told the pastor, "Today is the last day I'll be involved with the Baptist Church. I'm not going to get involved with the Baptist Church anymore because they don't follow the teaching in the Bible." Then Tsee and I drove home and never dealt with the Baptist Church again. I was traumatized like someone torn into little pieces.

I felt like Joseph, who went through emotional turmoil when his brothers betrayed him, threw him into a pit, and sold him into slavery. I did not hate the brother who accused us that day, but his calling me a fake felt like a knife in my back. It was a painful ending to something we had started with so much zeal and hope. We started that church in February 2015, and Tsee and I drove away in June 2016.

God taught us a heartbreaking yet valuable lesson through that attack, as he did with Joseph. Joseph had done no wrong against his brothers, but they betrayed him anyway. We had done no wrong to this brother. I had prayed for him and his entire family, and they were all healed. I had not done anything wrong to the church. I was praying for people, sharing Jesus, and trying to help them. It was not wrongdoing that brought us persecution but rather doing good. Through pain, we learned that "Yea, and all that will live godly in Christ Jesus shall suffer persecution: (2 Timothy 3:12 KJV).

And despite all that Joseph had to go through—betrayal, false accusation, temptations, and more—he somehow realized that what his brothers meant for evil, God used for good. I realized that persecution always spreads the Gospel. Whether we were being mocked at a public festival, on YouTube, or falsely accused in front of a church, God used it all to spread the Gospel. Like the days of the early Church, after Jesus ascended and went to Heaven, the church spread because of persecution. The Scripture says, ". . . And at that time there was a great persecution against the church which was at Jerusalem; and they were all scattered abroad throughout the regions of Judaea and Samaria, except the apostles. Therefore they that were scattered abroad went every where preaching the word" (Acts 8:1,4 KJV). Everybody left

Jerusalem. They all fled because of persecution and preached the Word of God as they went—that's how the church spread.

In December 2014, Prophet Yang told us, "God anointed you with the gift of healing and miracles. Six months from now, you will lay hands on the sick, and they will be healed." Six months later, I was indeed laying hands on the sick and seeing them healed. I was also leaving the Baptist church. The prophet told me when God chooses a person to perform a specific task for His Kingdom, Satan will use every force available to prevent the person's success. I just didn't realize Satan could use other Christians—and even denominational structures—to try to do so.

Soon, with that attack and the church-planting and outreach experiences "under our belt," the next part of God's prophecy through Prophet Yang began to unfold. He said, "In your lifetime, you will see many dead people raised from the dead, and you will be the first Hmong international evangelist to travel all over the world, preaching before thousands of people. Furthermore, in three years, you will be a pastor."

After leaving the Baptist church in June 2016, God brought us the right people and connections to start a spirit-filled, non-denominational church in January 2017. We called it The Church of Living God International. Within three years, I had become a pastor, and our international ministry went into motion. What we would see in India, Vietnam, and Thailand would blow our minds.

And Joseph dreamed a dream, and he told it his brethren: and they hated him yet the more. [18] And when they saw him [Joseph] afar off, even before he came near unto them, they conspired against him to slay him. [19] And they said one to another, Behold, this dreamer cometh. [20] Come now therefore, and let us slay him, and cast him into some pit, and we will say, Some evil beast hath devoured him: and we shall see what will become of his dreams. (Genesis 37:5, 18-20 KJV, brackets added)

> *But as for you, ye thought evil against me [Joseph speaking about his brother's conspiracy]; but God meant it unto good, to bring to pass, as it is this day, to save much people alive. (Genesis 50:20 KJV, brackets added)*

> *He sent a man before them, even Joseph, who was sold for a servant: [18] Whose feet they hurt with fetters: he was laid in iron: [19] Until the time that his word came: the word of the Lord tried him. (Psalm 105:17-19 KJV)*

God showed Joseph a dream, but He did not show him the persecution that would accompany the process of the dream coming to fruition. Prophet Yang told us we would lay hands on the sick, but he said nothing about a Christian brother betraying us. There may be tests, trials, and betrayals, but the Word of the Lord remains true. What the devil means for evil, God can use for good to save many people and accomplish His purpose for your life. Through persecution, His plan progressively unfolds.

CHAPTER 8: NEW TERRITORIES, NEW LEVELS

We sat waiting but couldn't overcome the nervous tension to look at each other. In silence, we could hear each other's hearts beat. Finally, the doctor entered the room.

"I'm so sorry," he said with a straight face. "The cells are cancerous, and the cancer has spread from your stomach."

"What can I do?" my uncle muttered in desperation, his eyes filled with fear.

"At this point, it's stage four. I would advise you to begin speaking with your family and getting things in order."

"What . . . I . . . I mean . . . How long do I have?"

"I would say four months."

My uncle was a Believer—a Christian—but he left that office bewildered that day. Anyone would have struggled with such devastating news, but seeing my uncle like that was difficult to handle. My father died when I was three, and my uncle always tried to show us love. He had seen his share of calamity, having survived the communist invasion of our home country in 1975 and our subsequent forced stay in a refugee camp. It was before coming to the refugee camp that he accepted Jesus Christ as his Savior. I did not believe in God then, but I appreciated my uncle's care and concern for us.

After leaving the refugee camp in Thailand, my uncle went to a Baptist seminary in Minnesota. He was the first Hmong person to become a Baptist minister and open a Hmong Baptist church. Still, the news of his cancer would test and change his faith forever because the Baptist church did not believe in healing, miracles, or other workings of the Holy Spirit.

After his diagnosis, a Spirit-filled Hmong minister came to visit him. He laid his hands on my uncle, prayed to God to heal him, and my uncle was cured. The doctors couldn't understand it, but my uncle was healed. He is still alive today, and that's why he believes in miracles and supports the things happening in our ministry now—even though he's a Baptist preacher and never formally studied the gifts of the Holy Spirit (1 Corinthians 12:4-7).

My uncle's acceptance of Jesus Christ and his decision to be a minister has affected my life and my brothers. My older brother also became a Baptist minister before I became a Christian. And after my conversion, my uncle encouraged some reluctant Baptist pastors to accept my ministry, specifically some reluctant ministers in Vietnam we would encounter after traveling to India.

***

The trip to India was unexpected. Tsee and I did not anticipant what awaited us in India, Vietnam, and Thailand. We had just started The Church of the Living God International in January 2017 in De Pere, Wisconsin. We were excited to launch a spirit-filled church that would not restrict the Holy Spirit's work—where miracles and healings could occur. We paid very little to use a building that seated 150 people. The pastor there also believed in the gifts of the Holy Spirit. He was a former Assembly of God pastor and agreed to let us use the building. We were finally going to have a Mark 16:17-18 church:

> And these signs will follow those who believe: In My name they will cast out demons; they will speak with new tongues; they will take up serpents; and if they drink anything deadly, it will

by no means hurt them; they will lay hands on the sick, and they will recover. (Mark 16:17-18 NKJV)

But then, all of a sudden, God said go to India. And unlike my uncle, who supported the healing and miracles that were happening in our ministry and encouraged other pastors to do the same, some Hmong pastors here in the United States had already told many churches in India, Laos, Thailand, Australia, France, and Vietnam not to open their doors to us. They did not believe Mark 16:17-18. Also, I had my own reasons to question the trip and was hesitant to accept the invitation.

From: jai <pjai@book.net>
To: jsalad <jsalad@book.net>
Sent: Date: Monday, January 17, 2017 09:15:33 EST
Subject: Invitation to India

Dear Pastor Salad,

You don't know me. I'm Pastor Jai, a pastor in India. I heard of you through a pastor friend of mine in Appleton and have seen your videos on YouTube and Facebook. God is doing many healings and miracles in your ministry, and we need that in India. I would like you to come to my country and help us pray for the sick. The people need real help. They need the power of God. Will you come?

Re: Invitation to India
From: jsalad <jsalad@book.net>
To: jai <pjai@book.net>

Greetings, Pastor Jai, in Jesus' name. My wife and I thank God for all the healings and miracles. The Holy Spirit is real. But I just became a pastor a few days ago, so I don't know how to teach or preach well yet. I'm just learning. I don't know how to pray, either. But I will pray to God to see if it's His will for us to come to India. Thank you for contacting me. I will get back to you.

In Christ,
Salad

Salad Vang

***

"Come and help us," they shouted silently with their eyes. They were all lined up—one behind each other—bound hand and foot. The chaotic rhythm I heard was the sound of a chain gang of slaves. They moved sluggishly, marking time with rattling and clanging from every step. They dredged through a valley in India, sandwiched by two mountains that each had a huge statue of Buddha on their top.

It was a dream so real I couldn't ignore it. The people looked so oppressed and weighed down in chains. I awoke and said, "Oh, God, if this a sign from You for me to go to India, then give me another sign or the same dream again." Then, the second night I had the same dream, and the third night—the same dream. I could not discount God's voice. It was clear that He wanted us to go to India. I told God, "Okay, I will go."

I learned that it was not unusual for God to communicate His will through dreams and visions. People in the Bible had visions and dreams where God's angels spoke to them and told them what to do, giving them direction. In Acts 16:9-10, Paul had a vision that made it clear he should go to Macedonia to preach the gospel. ""During the night Paul had a vision of a man of Macedonia standing and begging him, "Come over to Macedonia and help us." After Paul had seen the vision, we got ready at once to leave for Macedonia, concluding that God had called us to preach the gospel to them" (Acts 16:9-10 NIV). The man in the dream called him because people were crying out for help. Paul had to do God's will and give them the message of the Gospel of Jesus.

So after the third night of dreaming the same dream, I called the pastor and said, "Okay. It is the will of God. We're coming." My dreams were direction and confirmation. The pastor agreed, and we set a date for the trip.

But we still had a challenge. We only had two hundred dollars; that was all the money we had. How were we going to go to India, Vietnam, and

Thailand? I wondered who would take care of us. And what about my bills and student loans? We had to trust God and go. My mother-in-law would watch the children, but there was still another problem.

I didn't know how to teach or preach. Yes, I had prayed for the sick before, but I didn't want to be the featured speaker in a conference or church meeting and not know how to preach. What was I going to do? I asked God for help, and He put me back in dream training.

Every night, I would dream, and in my dreams, God would teach me how to pray, do deliverance, heal the sick, and preach and teach—in my dreams! Sometimes, I would wake up not remembering anything. But my wife would have recorded me talking in my sleep. I would listen in amazement, not having remembered what God had said. This kept happening until we went to India. I would have to act in faith and believe God to help me preach and teach His people.

***

We arrived in Mumbai, India, exhausted. We tried to sleep, but after about thirty minutes of restlessness, they showed up. God opened Tsee's eyes, and she saw demons on top of the hotel. I sensed their presence the same moment she saw them, and then I saw them too.

They were looking down at us—some big, some small, the sizes of trees, houses, and small buildings. They just stared—hovering and moving around on top of the hotel and over our room. They were shaped like the bodies of Hindu idols, and there were so many of them. It was like looking at a swarm of Hindu statues and goddesses—Shiva, Fati, and elephants. And they were expecting us. They were the local principalities, watching and staring with big, black eyeballs looking down on us and announcing that we had entered their territory and they would be watching us.

It seemed the odds were against us. The principalities were monitoring us, and some pastors from the United States had already told the pastors in Vietnam and Thailand not to accept us. I was a new pastor and didn't know how to preach and teach well, but we had to obey in faith.

The same night we saw the vision of the principalities I had to preach. When the time came, the Word of God just came out. What the Holy Spirit did was amazing. Usually, a preacher reads a script, but when I started to speak, the Holy Spirit helped me preach, and the words flowed out of me. I remembered the words in the Bible, and I preached without reading a script. It all just came out.

And there were miracle healings. The sick were healed, the blind saw, and the deaf heard. People possessed by demons were delivered, and many received the Holy Spirit. We had never seen anything of that magnitude before. Through the teaching, many came to know Jesus for the first time and received salvation. It was a mighty move of God.

We stayed in India for two weeks and then went to Vietnam for two weeks. In Vietnam, I taught and preached for almost twenty-four hours nonstop. After finally sleeping, I woke up, and they asked me to preach some more. It was February 2017, and we were in the mountains of Vietnam, where it was cold. The mosquitoes and the weather were against us, there were gaps and holes in the house walls, and you had to go outside in the freezing cold to get to the toilet. It was very uncomfortable, and there were moments we wanted to go home, but we knew we had to do God's work. And it was worth it because we saw miracles happen again. God touched so many people by the power of His Spirit. It was undeniable. Hindus, Buddhists, and Shamanists saw God's healing power through the name of Jesus.

Thailand was next.

***

"Before I preach, anybody who needs healing, come up here, and I will pray for you. A few people came forward, one of them a woman with a visible problem with one of her hands.

Do you believe Jesus can heal you?" I asked her in front of the hundred or so people that were there that night.

"Yes."

"Mark 16:18 says lay hands on the sick and they shall be healed." I put my hand on her wrist and continued. "In Jesus' name, be open. Hand open. Believe it." I said to her. "Jesus is in you. Jesus can do it. Believe it."

She tried opening her hand for about two minutes, and then—boom—it opened. Her arm stretched out, and all the scar tissue was gone. She was cured.

We were in Bangkok, Thailand, at a prisoner's church. This woman was from Vietnam, but she spoke Hmong. She had come to the prisoner's church for shelter. But four years before that night, she had been involved in a motor vehicle accident and fallen off her motorcycle. She broke the bones in her wrist and forearm and could not open her hand.

She had suffered from immobility in her hand and scars for four years, and everyone there knew her story. So when they saw God's power heal her and stretch out her arm, they all came and gave their lives to Jesus. And after she came up front, everybody got healed—everybody!

These miracles didn't take place without opposition. Many of the preachers in Thailand had been told not to let us preach. But there was a pastor who was a leader in the United Pentecostal Churches of Thailand who spoke Hmong. He accepted me and didn't listen to the naysayers. The other pastors did not want him to accept me. They didn't want him to be with me or bring me to their church to pray for the sick, preach, or do deliverance. They didn't believe in Mark 16:18 or take any outsiders, but he ignored them. He had seen YouTube videos of our ministry and believed.

While still in Bangkok, we faced more opposition three days before our trip back home to the United States. This time it was backlash and spiritual retaliation from the principalities and powers through witchcraft. A dark black line appeared on my thumb, like a needle that went from the tip to the bottom of my thumbnail. That night it turned red and began to swell. The pain was so excruciating that I couldn't sleep, and after two days, my thumbnail became dark purple. On the third day, it looked like the nail was going to fall off. We knew right away it was witchcraft. It was those demons in India and Vietnam—the Buddha demons and witchcraft in Thailand. They all gathered and tried to hurt and attack us for the work that we had done for Jesus. Then Tsee also developed a skin rash. It was like leprosy, white, flaky, and scaly on her hands and face. It looked horrible. It took a week or so for us to get back to normal. We had never experienced anything like this before, and after we got back home, we learned that we should have fasted and prayed more before the trip.

***

Now we know to fast and pray before we go, and we bind demons before entering a territory. We cast them out of the city, the streets, and the country. That's what you need to do before you go. You must bind and cast out the principalities, evil spirits, and powers. Now, when we go, we don't see the same problems.

Despite the opposition and attacks, God saved, delivered, and healed so many people in India, Vietnam, and Thailand. We returned home knowing that God's power was real and seeing God do things at a greater magnitude than we had ever seen before.

We were so excited we forgot about the bills and student loans we had left behind, but we were in for a surprise. A few weeks after our return, I went to the mailbox and saw a letter informing me that my student loans from medical school had a zero balance. That was a hundred thousand dollars, all taken care of! I got down on my knees and started crying and thanking God. I don't know how it happened. The letter

The Sword, the Serpent, and the Spiritual Realm

said it had been paid, and I had a zero balance. And it was a good thing because we had paid for the trip to India, Vietnam, and Thailand with a credit card. And there was more.

God would surprise again. Some weeks later, we got an email about our income taxes. We received a refund—an amount we had never received before. We thought that we would owe taxes. But when the accountant emailed the return details, we saw a refund of $22,000.00. I thought it was a mistake, so I called the accountant and said this had never happened to us before. I asked, "You've been our accountant for so many years, and what is this? Is this an error?" She responded, "No, it's not. It's your return."

We were supposed to pay, not get money, and we certainly did not expect to get $22,000.00. We had never received that kind of money from the Internal Revenue Service (IRS). We went to Asia in faith, with only $200.00, and God supplied more than we imagined. Financially, we didn't have anything before we left for the trip.

Then I remembered that before we left, I was still praying about the trip, and the snow came down. When I saw the snowfall, I heard the audible voice of God say, "Look at the snow. Do you see how much snow is coming down? That's how many blessings I'm blessing you with, and I'm going to bless you." That word came to pass after we got back. God is so faithful.

YouTube and Facebook videos led to an invitation to preach the gospel in three countries. Within two years after being saved, I had become a pastor and was seeing miraculous healings. The word of the Lord through Prophet Yang was coming to pass. We saw so many healings, salvations, deliverances, and people being filled with the Holy Spirit.

It was miracle after miracle in all three countries. The crippled walked, the blind saw, the deaf heard, the sick were healed, and demons were cast out in all three countries. People who believed in Buddha gave their lives to Jesus. Hindus and Shamanists were also converted after they saw the power of God to heal them, and they believed that Jesus was more powerful than their gods.

It was so amazing; it's hard to believe some pastors tried to prevent others from accepting us. Still, God touched and changed people's lives. His word is true.

> He said to them, "Go into all the world and preach the gospel to all creation. [16] Whoever believes and is baptized will be saved, but whoever does not believe will be condemned. [17] And these signs will accompany those who believe: In my name they will drive out demons; they will speak in new tongues; [18] they will pick up snakes with their hands; and when they drink deadly poison, it will not hurt them at all; they will place their hands on sick people, and they will get well."
> (Mark 16:15-18 NIV)

CHAPTER 9: FOOLISH THINGS

Peering down, I could see the creek's flowing water in the valley between us and the other mountain. Then, my eyes moved up to the other mountain top. It was about fifty yards away. I took in everything I was seeing but wondered what was going on.

Why were my hands and feet tied in ropes—why was I being held captive? And who had done this? I looked up and saw a king and queen, each wearing a crown and seated on a horse. I noticed a few other people being held captive with me. We were facing the other mountain, soldiers patiently standing over us. It was as if we were waiting for more people to come.

I looked at the other mountaintop again and saw men riding horses like a royal battalion charging into war. But what was more shocking was my husband, Salad, was leading the way. He rode a white horse and had a spear in his left hand.

He stopped and threw the spear towards our mountain. I reacted; I was really upset, and the other captives with me were in shock because it seemed like an impossible distance for a spear to reach. The king laughed in mockery, saying, "This man is so dumb."

When I heard the word dumb, I thought, "I can't believe that's my husband. What has he done? This is ridiculous. Here we are, being held captive, and he and a bunch of men are on their horses, riding pretty fast, at a far distance, and there he goes. He throws the spear?" It seemed impossible that it could reach us or even hurt anyone from that distance. "Why wouldn't the king laugh," I thought.

As the king continued laughing, we saw the spear invade our mountaintop. In between laughs, he looked at the spear as it approached. We all looked at it, and as the spear passed the king, it touched his left arm only slightly. No one expected what happened next—he exploded into pieces. The queen, all the soldiers, and all of us froze in amazement. Wait a minute? What's going on? What is this?

Salad wasn't looking so dumb anymore. It was unbelievable.

I awoke from this dream and understood God was speaking to me about mockery. Salad had posted several videos from our trip to India, Vietnam, and Thailand on Facebook and YouTube. The miracles people saw resulted in controversy from everywhere—young, old, women, and men all made fun of us or said the miracles were fake. Some even threatened to hurt us. They ridiculed us on radio and social media and wrote thousands of negative comments. And most of them were Believers—other lukewarm Christians were laughing and attacking my husband.

I was so confused. I wondered if something was going on with Salad. Why were all these people attacking? I thought maybe something was wrong because the way he prays is not normal. All the mockery and persecution caused me to start questioning what was happening. But when I had this dream, I knew God was reassuring me and telling me people had never seen what God was doing in our ministry, and that's why they were laughing. They were ignorant of the power of God. The dream confirmed it and built my confidence again.

After that, I didn't care what people were saying or doing. My trust was in the Lord because he had given me an understanding of what was happening in the spiritual realm—what was really happening. Demons, their devices, and their territories were being destroyed. God was using my husband.

For we wrestle not against flesh and blood, but against principalities, against powers, against the rulers of the darkness of this world, against spiritual wickedness in high places. (Ephesians 6:12 KJV)

The Sword, the Serpent, and the Spiritual Realm

I decided not to pay attention to anybody around us anymore. Their negative comments, ridicule, and mockery didn't matter—even if they were Christians. I understood it was possible to be a Believer and not understand or have experience with the Holy Spirit and the spiritual realm. Still, many people are hungry for the power of the Holy Spirit. They want something real and life-changing, and the Holy Spirit is real and indeed life-changing if we open up to experience Him instead of laughing at what we don't understand. God will give those who are hungry for Him what they ask for:

> For every one that asketh receiveth; and he that seeketh findeth; and to him that knocketh it shall be opened. [11] If a son shall ask bread of any of you that is a father, will he give him a stone? or if he ask a fish, will he for a fish give him a serpent? [12] Or if he shall ask an egg, will he offer him a scorpion? [13] If ye then, being evil, know how to give good gifts unto your children: how much more shall your heavenly Father give the Holy Spirit to them that ask him? (Luke 11:10-13 KJV)

And what many Believers must understand is what we don't understand often looks foolish to us, but if it's in God's Word, that doesn't change the fact that it's real. First Corinthians 1:27 says, "God hath chosen the foolish things of the world to confound the wise; and God hath chosen the weak things of the world to confound the things which are mighty." God can use the unwise to shame the wise. He can use things that are ridiculous, and it was ridiculous how Salad was praying, and people were being healed and delivered. It was just unbelievable—but it was God!

I needed this newfound confidence not only for our work in the field but also for our work in the local church. We returned from our trip to India, Vietnam, and Thailand in March 2017. We didn't travel internationally again until February 2018, but other issues were about to ensue—not from unbelievers—from Believers in the church.

Just before our trip to India, Vietnam, and Thailand, we opened a church in De Pere, Wisconsin, in January 2017. There were only a few members when we started, but new people joined, and it grew. While we were happy for growth, the new members brought challenges; they brought their Hmong traditions and culture.

***

"Pastor, the church is growing," my assistant pastor grinned. "There are many new people, and there are some things Deacon Fang, Treasurer Lau, and I would like to discuss with you, please."

"Okay, what is it? "

"Well, you know our customs. We have a lot of new Hmong people, and they want to honor their loved ones when they die."

"What do you mean by honor?"

"Well . . . since we have a lot of Hmong people in the church. When someone dies, we should do three-day, four-day, and five-day funerals like our people do, not these one-day funerals like Americans. We are Hmong people—Christian or not. And we need to kill cows so everyone has enough to eat. We want the people to stay in the church, right?"

"When a Believer dies, they are going to be with Christ. That's what we should focus on, not the type of food. And you know the cows are also an offering for the ancestors. That's idol worship, and Christians don't do that."

"Pastor, I think you need to reconsider," Deacon Fang chimed in. Some older members complain that our traditions are not being honored. They say you have changed and no longer respect our culture. You don't want that do you?"

The Sword, the Serpent, and the Spiritual Realm

"Deacon, seeing the Lord is cause for celebration. The older women want to carry on with loud, scary wailing and crying. That's not what a Christian's funeral should be about. No, we don't cry scary cries. We cry to God. We thank God because the person now is in a good place after death."

"This isn't going to work, Pastor. We have tried to talk with you. Don't say we didn't tell you so when people start leaving."

My assistant pastor, treasurer, and one of the deacons had revealed one of the strongest spirits that fight the New Testament Church—the spirit of tradition. Some church members were more committed to their culture and traditions than Jesus and His Word. They weren't interested in what the Word of God had to say about these matters. They wanted their cultural funerals and New Year's celebrations—even if they would invite demons into their lives and the church.

In Hmong culture, multiple-day funerals involve offering cows to ancestors, along with whiskey and money. And for the Hmong New Year's celebration, they wear traditional clothes that have witchcraft symbols, dragons, and snakes. They wanted to wear these clothes to church and celebrate that day as the New Year. We said no, we don't do that, but then they caused division because they didn't get what they wanted—and those three—the assistant pastor, treasurer, and deacon conspired together to strike a final blow to the church I would have to rely on God to overcome.

They wanted to please the people, hold on to their Hmong traditions, and mix paganism with the Church, and they were not happy that I would not give in. So the assistant pastor, deacon, and treasured sabotaged us. They took money from the church to have dinner at the restaurant. That night they conspired; they wrote each other cheques for the church's bank account—$20,000.00, $10,000.00, $5,000.00—then took the money and ran. We didn't know until we checked the church bank account one day, and all the money was gone. I talked to my mentor pastor and asked what we should do. He said I should call the police and report them to the authorities as thieves. I was reluctant but told him I would pray about it. And as I prayed, God spoke to my heart and told me not to get a lawyer or get the police involved, just forgive them. It was hard because I was hurt. But I forgave them, and I did not get a lawyer or the police. I forgave them.

After I forgave them, God blessed me and my family with good health, peace, love, and joy. People in the church started giving more, and God blessed us with land. I'm so glad I didn't go the traditional lawyer route—I went the God route. They wanted their traditions more than Jesus. Satan uses tradition to attack the church and God's people.

> *Thus you nullify the word of God by your tradition that you have handed down. And you do many things like that." (Mark 7:13 NIV)*

But tradition and people-pleasing was not the only challenge we had in De Pere. Some members who spoke in tongues were even worse than those in the Baptist church who didn't believe in the Holy Spirit. They did not match their zeal for the Spirit with knowledge of the Word, so they had weird ideas about the Spirit that were not Scriptural. They prophesied things that were not true and confused people because they didn't know the Word of God. They told people things like, "Just listen to the voice. Whatever the voice says, believe it." But they were listening to demonic voices thinking it was the Holy Spirit. They lacked the discernment that comes from knowing and exercising the Word of God (Hebrews 5:14), so they became like soothsayers and fortune tellers who allowed devils to speak through them. The spirit of divination had entered them. Because of this, so many Southeast Asian churches are now filled with false prophets. There are some true prophets, but most are now chasing after power instead of a relationship with Jesus, and they're lost. They are not rooted in the Word of God.

> *For every one that useth milk is unskilful in the word of righteousness: for he is a babe. ^{14} But strong meat belongeth to them that are of full age, even those who by reason of use have their senses exercised to discern both good and evil. (Hebrews 5:13-14 KJV)*

We opened other Spirit-filled churches where there was speaking in tongues, deliverance, and healing in St. Paul in April 2017, Brooklyn Park in June 2017, and Madison in 2018. Like the church in De Pere, each had its own challenges.

In St. Paul and Brooklyn Park, the church leaders could drink beer, get drunk, and post it on Facebook. They participated in Shaman feasts, eating food offered to demons. They also committed adultery and touched women's chests and stomachs while praying for them. They would push people down when they prayed for them instead of letting the Holy Spirit do His work. They wanted to appear as if they were powerful, and people were falling out when they prayed for them. We spoke against it, telling them adultery was a sin against God and their wives. They didn't listen. They said they were involved with other women to attract customers for their real estate businesses and financial investments. They thought they needed to eat, drink, and engage in sinful behavior to bring those people into their business deals. But they should have talked to them about Jesus and the Gospel. We had to remove them from leadership.

> Now the works of the flesh are evident, which are: adultery, fornication, uncleanness, lewdness, [20] idolatry, sorcery, hatred, contentions, jealousies, outbursts of wrath, selfish ambitions, dissensions, heresies, [21] envy, murders, drunkenness, revelries, and the like; of which I tell you beforehand, just as I also told you in time past, that those who practice such things will not inherit the kingdom of God. (Galatians 5:19-22 NKJV)

These problems are in many churches today. They have focused more on people-pleasing and welcome anything into God's church—even Halloween. Why? The more members, the more money. But by pleasing the people, the people are not being saved—not truly saved. They are still living in sin, gambling, beating their wives, cursing, and more because the conviction of the Word of God is not in their church. The preacher no longer preaches about sin, repentance, or letting go of the past. So the people don't know what it means to deny themselves, follow Christ, and be renewed in Him. They don't know what it is to carry their cross and crucify their flesh. The result is a very shallow Christianity.

We have planted several churches and ministered in even more churches, and we see that many local churches are becoming more like social clubs. People come to church to eat, talk about life, and party; there are so many church clubs now. For example, we went to a large Hmong church in Carolina. They have over a thousand members, and there are so many activities and clubs. They've got a women's club for makeup, a club for cooking, a club for playing golf, and others. The day we went, the members signed up at the church to see which of the twenty-five clubs they would attend. They even had a club for sewing traditional Hmong clothes—every kind of club you can think of, they've got it.

And while the Church is supposed to be a community of believers, it's not supposed to be a social club. The Church community should be focused on pleasing Christ and winning others to Him. It should focus on sound doctrine, fellowship, communion, prayer, and worship (Acts 2:42). If we are not careful, the modern-day Church will become pagan, mixing culture, tradition, and ancestral worship with Christianity. And that means people who are sick, demonized, tortured by the devil, poor, and depressed will not get what they need to be free in Christ. Paganism and mixture open the door for evil spirits to come in and torment them. But they do not know that.

We must stay in the Word and prayer so our eyes can be open to the wiles and devices of the enemy against the Church. Satan attacks some churches with rebellion, resulting in rebellious leaders and church splits. Other churches are attacked with witchcraft or a Jezebel spirit that seeks to manipulate leadership and the people. Witchcraft can sometimes operate by bringing a new member who seems very helpful but has wrong motives. They seem very spiritual and say things like, "Oh, this is my first day at your church. Can I be a helper? I know the Bible, I speak in tongues, I'm anointed. I have believed in God for fifteen years. I want to be your deacon; I want to be your assistant pastor. Can I do that?" They are saying things like that on the first day. I realized that's a wrong spirit. If they get access, they can cause many problems.

In other churches, there's a spirit of division, tradition, gossip, deception, or adultery. And adultery is very big in Asian churches. Everywhere we go, we see and hear husbands having mistresses. The enemy is attacking, and we cannot remain ignorant of his devices.

When we first came to Jesus, we were naïve. We thought everyone was holy and believed what the Bible said about the Holy Spirit. But we quickly learned that was not the case. Satan has gained a foothold in many churches, and his evil works must be destroyed. But if the believers and church leaders don't have their eyes open, the enemy will further his agenda. He (the enemy) comes to steal, kill, and destroy, but Jesus came to give us real life—freedom in our spirits, souls, and bodies. That is what Jesus came to do. So we cannot let the devil continue to work his evil works of witchcraft, seduction, and division. If we believe the Bible, we will cast out devils, lay hands on the sick, and walk in the power of the Holy Spirit. We will lay down our traditions, and fully embrace the Cross.

First Corinthians 1:27 says, "God hath chosen the foolish things of the world to confound the wise; and God hath chosen the weak things of the world to confound the things which are mighty." The healings and miracles that took place looked foolish to some. They mocked and ridiculed. Still, many lives were changed, and souls were saved. God can use the foolish things of this world to confound the wisdom of the wise, but He doesn't want foolishness in His Church.

All things are lawful for me, but all things are not helpful. All things are lawful for me, but I will not be brought under the power of any. [13] *Foods for the stomach and the stomach for foods, but God will destroy both it and them. Now the body is not for sexual immorality but for the Lord, and the Lord for the body. (1 Corinthians 6:12-13 NKJV)*

CHAPTER 10: MANY NATIONS, MANIFESTATION, AND MIRACLES

The "voom vroom" of motorcycles, "beep beep" of taxis, "honk honk" of cars, "ring ring" of bike bells, and the "flip flop" of feet hitting the pavement all share the same road on Vietnamese streets. And to the typical American who has never lived in a major city, it sounds like chaos. And when you add the occasional elderly person riding a regular bike or a woman with two children on a single motorbike, it sounds like discord to an untraveled ear and resembles the very definition of danger. Indeed, Vietnam is a different world for the average American.

But it's not only the sounds of the constant traffic and differences in understanding personal space but also the smells. Vietnam is home to some of the world's most beautiful people and delicious dishes. It also has the pungent aromas of spicy marinated grilled octopus, durian, also known as "stinky fruit," fermented fish sauce, and thang co, a stew of horse meat, horse intestines, and local spices. These smells fill the same streets already fragranced by vehicular and industrial exhaust. So when an American member of our mission team was overwhelmed, we were not surprised.

The mission field can be intense, especially when it's not missions mixed with vacations. Our mission trip was to seven countries in only three weeks. It was as demanding as it was fruitful, and we warned her beforehand.

> "Sister, this trip is going to require endurance. It's not going to be easy." I warned. "We are always going to be on the run. You may get weak; we will always be working, and there's going to

> be little rest. It's going to be like a marathon. Are you sure you can take it?"
>
> "I can take it," she confidently replied. "I have perseverance, and I want to climb the mountain."
>
> "Okay, I just want you to know it's not going to be easy, and this is your first time traveling."
>
> "I know, I know. I can do it."

Any international trip requires planning, specifically visas, immunizations, flights, housing, etc. But this trip was to seven countries (Vietnam, Thailand, Burma, India, Rwanda, Kenya, and Ethiopia)—so much coordination was necessary. The seven of us prepared for the trip and arrived in our first country, Vietnam, in February 2018.

Vietnam

> "What's that smell? I'm going to throw up," she said with repulsion. "The food and the water aren't clean. I can't eat or drink anything."

Tsee and I were afraid she would not have enough energy. She even said the fruit on the street was not clean. So, she did not take anything in, and we were worried that the situation would slow us down in the work of God. She only ate a little bit of cookies or chips while we were in Vietnam, but God showed her compassion. Several things prevented us from doing any mission work in Vietnam, including a lot of persecution from the government, which made the first few days of the trip easier for her. Next, we went to Thailand.

The Sword, the Serpent, and the Spiritual Realm

Thailand

It was as if we were traveling nonstop from village to village, and there were miracles everywhere in Thailand. One of the first involved a pregnant mother's brain-dead baby. The doctors were going to remove the baby from her womb, but we fasted and prayed for three days, and the baby's brain became normal. The mother had a normal delivery, and her baby was fine. God turned it around and worked a miracle, but it took prayer and fasting. That dead baby came back to life in its mother's womb.

We continued to see many miracle healings, deliverances, and salvations. In one Thai village, thirteen Buddhist worshippers along with Shaman idol worshippers, came to Christ. In a town called Tak, Thailand, there was a church with ten people, but when we went there, hundreds of people from all over Thailand suddenly gathered outside. There was no room to sit, so they listened from outside, and there were healings, deliverances, salvations, and boom! It was like a Pentecost revival.

We went to the border of Thailand and Laos, and hundreds of communists crossed the border and got saved, healed, delivered, and filled with the Holy Spirit in the meeting. It was huge!

Then we went to Kamphaeng Phet, about a day's drive west of the border. We saw healings, miracles, and Buddhist worshippers coming to Christ. Then we went to Chaing Mai, followed by Chiang Rai up north, and saw the same thing. Unbelievers were coming to Christ. There were salvations, healings, deliverances, and huge miracles. For example, we saw a little girl who was born crippled and unable to walk who started walking. The deaf heard; the blind saw!

God healed that little girl in a church called the Billy Cole Pentecostal Church in Thailand. It seats over 5,000 people. They never allowed anybody that is not in their church or any non-Pentecostal minister to preach. It was the first time they allowed somebody not licensed in the

Pentecostal church to minister. So they were amazed when they saw this little girl walking and people being saved all over Thailand. Denominational barriers were broken by the power of the Holy Spirit. Myanmar, formally named Burma, was next.

Myanmar

We went to a church and two orphanage facilities in Yangon, Myanmar. They were hungry for God and ready to put their faith to work. God was faithful to His Word again—many were saved, healed, and delivered under a strong anointing in Jesus' name. Our next country was India.

India

We went to Nagpur, India, to do a grand opening of a church we had built. It's a two-story, big, beautiful worship building surrounded by Hindus and anti-Christians. In Nagpur, Buddha and Hindu statues filled the city with very few churches in between. They were visual representations that those strongholds were still rooted in the region, and they were attacking the churches in the region. We also went to Mumbai, and again, so many people were saved, healed, and delivered in Jesus' name.

Rwanda

Africa was next, specifically Rwanda, where a genocide occurred in 1994. Hutu militias massacred an estimated 800,000 people from the Tutsi tribe. We could hear and feel the spirits all over, crying out for help. So much blood has been spilled, and there was a lot of witchcraft and voodoo. The witches and voodoo doctors knew we were coming because the churches put signs everywhere and did radio advertisements announcing, "Pastor Salad Vang is coming."

Then, the witch doctors sent demons to attack us at the hotel. We saw them enter the windows and shadows at midnight but were not scared.

We went up the mountain the next day, and the demons tried to stop us. It rained as we went up the mountain, and our truck almost fell off a steep ridge. But when we got there, many people gave their lives to Jesus. Thirty-four souls were saved that night, and many were healed and delivered. Glory to God! -It was powerful! But the opposition wasn't over.

When we left the mountain people and started our return to the hotel, it was so dark and raining hard. By the time we saw the flood on the mountain, our truck had died in the middle of the road. Somebody had to come from the city to fix the car at night. As we waited in the darkness of night, we could hear all the evil demon spirits. It was scary but also exciting to be doing the will of God. It was a weird adventure, and Kenya was next.

Kenya

There was a different turn of events in Kenya. A bishop conned us and stole the money we gave to prepare for the crusade. They stole all the money, and everything was canceled abruptly. It was a demonic conspiracy; it was witchcraft. They even threatened us. It was like a movie. It was surreal. So, nothing was done there because the devil and witchcraft influenced the church leader who was supposed to help us conduct the crusade. We continued to Ethiopia.

Ethiopia: Prophecy Manifested

It was the last country of our trip. God opened a door for us to talk to the leader of a church with over six million members. Usually, he wouldn't talk to anyone he didn't know on such short notice. But I went there, and the next day, I was sitting with many bishops, pastors, and leaders—well-known leaders of hundreds of churches. I was invited to preach with four or five other anointed preachers. I was the little Asian man there, and they were looking at me with a "Who is this Asian man?" expression. They had never seen an Asian preacher before in the fifty years of their crusade.

Some asked, "Oh, where are you from? Who are you? How many years are you a pastor? How big is your church?" I told them I had only been pastoring for one year, and the church was small. They looked at me like a nobody who should not have even been sitting with them.

When it was my turn to preach, the host pastor told me to pray for the sick. I preached and said, "Who has sickness in the body? Raise your hand. Put your hand where you need healing." About a million people were there, and hundreds of thousands raised their hands and put them where they hurt. I started casting out evil spirits and commanding sickness to go. Then, I asked, "Who is healed?" So many raised their hands and were cheering. Then, the other guest preachers were convinced that the little Asian preacher he had let preach had God.

They treated me differently after that. It was like a movie and a miracle. That's the first time in history that anybody from my country preached to one million people. God opened the door—I had only been a pastor for one year. How was this possible? We saw hundreds of thousands of people healed. We saw the Holy Ghost touch their hearts like a wind and heal them. Then, the other preachers and the bishops who had looked down on me could see that God was with me—the little Asian preacher from nowhere.

Prophet Yang had said, "Soon you will not only lay hands on people, but the words you speak out of your mouth will enable thousands to be healed." He continued, "God anointed you with the gift of healing and miracles." That portion of his prophecy had come to pass that day in Ethiopia. All glory belongs to God!

We returned from that seven-country trip in March 2018, seeing more of what God had prophesied come to pass. We didn't know that we would again see more of the prophecy unfold later that year.

The Sword, the Serpent, and the Spiritual Realm

***

Summer 2018

In June, we went to minister in Cairns and Innisfail, Australia, and so many shaman practitioners and idol worshippers got healed and delivered—eighteen people gave their lives to Jesus. The blind saw, the deaf heard, the crippled walked, and the sick were healed. It was powerful! Everyone who came to the barn shed meetings got healed and delivered for two days straight in Innisfail. Then we flew to Brisbane, Australia, and twenty-four idol worshippers gave their lives to Jesus. A family of five cut off all the demonic wrist ties from their wrists and ankles and gave their lives to Jesus. Again, everyone was healed at a farm shed meeting that day in Brisbane. The day before the miracle meeting in Brisbane, we were invited to a picnic at the park, and so many people gave their lives to Jesus. Also, many got healed and delivered in Jesus' name. It was a powerful move of God in Australia.

Then, a few people asked us to go to St. Paul, MN, to do a water baptism service. Afterward, they posted about it on Facebook. A Native Indian woman with breast cancer came for the service. After I prayed, she went to see her medical doctor, and the cancer was gone. Glory to God!

From there, my wife and I went to Atlanta, GA, to an African American church to minister, and so many people were healed and delivered from demonic oppression. The crippled walked, and the sick free were set free from unclean spirits of infirmity in Jesus' name.

Fall 2018

In September, my wife and I went to Haiti, where gangsters blocked our vehicle and asked us to pay a fee before we could move on. A lot of voodoo and witchcraft occurred at night near the hotel where we were staying, and many of Haiti's people were demonized and oppressed. There is so much violence and gang fighting. While in Haiti,

I preached on top of a voodoo master's temple, and hundreds of people gathered to listen to the salvation message. Thirty-four people were baptized the next day, and many were healed and delivered in Jesus' name as well.

Dubai and Philippines: Prophecy Manifested

In early October 2018, we went to Dubai, a rich and beautiful country, but its government only allowed church for a few hours on Friday—there were no Sunday services. But even in a few hours, we prayed and saw miracle healings and deliverance. When we "go into all the world and preach the gospel," God also sends signs of deliverance and healing to follow us (Mark 16:15-18). He is faithful to His Word.

We were planning to go to Pakistan after Dubai, but suddenly, God opened a door for us to go to Manila, Philippines. We didn't know it would be where another part of Prophet Yang's prophecy would be fulfilled. In 2014, Peter Yang said, "You're going to preach where Billy Graham preached." Manilla was that place.

When we got there, hundreds of thousands of people worshipped God in harmony—it was a beautiful sight to behold. I got to stand up and preach about salvation from Romans 10:13. Amazingly, I stood exactly where Billy Graham stood when he preached to hundreds of thousands of people there. It was the same pulpit, the same place, and the same stand. They told me Billy Graham had been there, and the Pope had too, preaching where I was standing. I was astounded. More of the prophecy had come to pass. God is faithful to His Word when we move in faith.

In General Santos City and Manila, Philippines, we witnessed Jesus heal, deliver, and save more people. We went to minister in Muslims territories up the mountains where ISIS were close by and many gave their lives to Jesus. It was a dangerous time, so soldiers with machine guns had to guard our outdoor crusade. There were various signs during the healings. For example, sicknesses were expelled when I drove them out with my hands, and the Holy Spirit led me to blow and breathe on others to drive out sickness, infirmity, and unclean spirits. Like Paul's handkerchiefs, my sports coat became a point of contact for healing. They had never seen anything like it before. Glory to God! As we continued to go, He continued to show Himself strong through powerful healings and signs.

A Spanish pastor in Menasha, WI, invited me to minister at their church, and there was a woman with terminal cancer. Doctors said she would die soon because they could not help her anymore. She came to the altar, and I said, "In the name of Jesus Christ, I command the cancer in this woman to leave now and never come back. Go!" She fell to the ground, and a few weeks later, she was completely cured. Her atheist medical doctor became a believer and was baptized six months later. Everyone got healed at the altar. It was amazing.

After that, in October, we went to minister in St. Louis, MO, in an African American church. Many of these churches had never invited an Asian preacher before. It was the Lord making the way and opening doors as prophesied by Brother Yang. Again, everyone who came to the altar got healed and delivered in Jesus' name. An African American woman who had been blind for two years was healed. After prayer, she could see almost thirty feet away, and everyone was amazed because they knew her situation well.

We went to Japan and South Korea in September and Vietnam and Thailand in November. In Japan and South Korea, evil spirits demonized many people due to idol worship and the sea spirits surrounding the islands. Many were sick and oppressed, but all who came to the altar got healed and delivered in Jesus' name. Glory to God!

In December, we went Fresno, Sacramento, and Merced, CA, where we ministered in Hmong churches. Again, God's power was present to heal and deliver, and many people were filled with the Holy Spirit. A White woman who had completely lost vision in her right eye was healed. Her vision became clear, and she began to cry out to God with joy. There was so much diversity in those services; people of all nationalities came, including Hispanics, African Americans, Hmong, Mien, Filipinos, Caucasians, and others—they were all gathered in these healing meetings.

God healed every one. Cancers and other incurable diseases were healed, the crippled walked, the deaf heard, the mute spoke, and more. For many people, when I placed my sports coat over their bodies and took it off, they were immediately healed (Acts 19:12)—it was so amazing. After posting videos of the healings on social media, Asian radio, local papers, and Facebook, they went viral. Hundreds of thousands commented on the videos, but many did so in the most negative ways. Some people made funny videos about me that were spreading on the Internet like crazy. I was all over the news in the USA and globally, especially in the Asian community. There were even Halloween customs of me for sale in some Asian stores.

A Year Later: 2019

Summer

We went to minister in Osseo, MI at a White church, and then to an African American church in Jackson, MI where many miracles took place. The blind saw, the deaf heard, and the crippled walked. God restored broken bones, and people were healed and delivered of depression, arthritis, pain, and the list goes on and on. Glory to God!

> "Would you like to walk?" I asked as she approached the altar. I was curious why a ten-year-old girl was on crutches.
>
> "Yes, I would like to walk."
>
> "What happened?"
>
> "I fractured my ankle."

"Okay, do you believe Jesus can heal you? "

"Yes."

"Be healed in Jesus' name and walk."

I took her cast and crutches off, and she started . . . slowly. At first, it was painful, but she kept walking—gradually, slowly, and then she started walking normally.

"What is the pain level now?" I asked.

"Zero!" she replied, and the church cheered.

The next day, she came back to that three-day revival wearing high heels. She had no pain, the fracture was gone, and her bones were restored. That little girl got healed in June 2018 in a White church in Michigan. We went to Michigan to preach in two churches. This one was in Osseo Michigan, and the other was an African American church in Jackson, Michigan.

In the Osseo church, there was a blind Caucasian woman. When I laid hands on her and declared, "Eyes be opened in Jesus' name," boom— she started to see. Everybody was amazed because she had been blind for many years. Then, another White woman came to the altar. She had been diagnosed with lung cancer, and scans had shown nodules in her lungs. She wanted Jesus to heal her, so I said, "Okay, in the name of Jesus Christ, cancer, go away from her! Be healed! Let her lungs be restored!" The next day, she went to see the doctor, and they retook a CT scan. She came back to the revival and told us the doctor said there was no cancer on her X-ray. It was gone, and there was medical proof that she had been healed.

Then, people with arthritis in their bodies, hands, and fingers were healed. Jesus healed whatever was ailing them. It was just amazing.

Everybody that came to the altar got healed—everybody! And they were all believers already, but they had infirmities from the enemy.

We went to an African American church in Jackson, Michigan, the same week. God healed people from ringing ears, deafness, blurry vision, back pain, arthritis, and more. Like the previous church, everybody who came to the altar got healed. They were already saved but still attacked with sickness, disease, and infirmity. So again, we saw miracles, healings, and deliverance for God's people.

We went to a Hispanic Church in Menasha, WI, and again, the signs and wonders were so amazing. People everywhere were falling in response to God's power. God is good. Praise the Lord!

In September we went to an African American church in Detroit, MI to minster and many more miracles took place. All got healed, many just by speaking the Word in Jesus' name. One woman just had a motor vehicle accident, and she was sitting in the pew wearing a cervical collar. I had come down from the dates and was on the preaching floor. commanded the pain to go, in Jesus' name and the damaged tissues in her body to be restored. Instantly, she was healed.

In November 2019, we returned to Vietnam and Thailand and saw more miracles. People were filled with the Holy Spirit and began to speak in tongues. This time, God's anointing on my life increased. There was a demonstration of God's power at a greater level. The glory of God made it hard for people to stand; they were falling everywhere. There was salvation, healing, and deliverance through the teaching and preaching of the kingdom of God and ministering the gifts of the Spirit.

By now, the lukewarm church in Vietnam was familiar with our ministry and incited persecution. On this trip, a lukewarm pastor threatened to call the police, but when he did, his child fell sick and could not breathe. He ended up calling us to pray for his child, and when God healed his child, he didn't call the police. We had someone keep watch at the door while I was preaching because of police threats—they wanted to take me to jail. We once had to flee a village at 3:00 AM by motorcycle to avoid being arrested and almost had to be let down a wall in a basket like Paul. They were going to take us to jail because missionaries and pastors were not allowed to go to these areas to preach. It was dangerous but exciting. We knew God was protecting us.

There were so many miracles, and the people were hungry for God. They would gather even though the threat of police harassment existed. In one village, over seventy people gave their lives to Jesus, and in one place in the mountains, unbelievers came to get healing for the first time. Idol worshippers came to Jesus in a communist country. That is fruit! They are hungry for God and getting filled with the Holy Spirit. Unlike so many that are lukewarm in America, they are on fire. There is so much fruit. That is why we continue to go to the nations, and we see more miracles than ever—the dead are raised in Jesus' name.

We even saw God move on the plane during our flight back to America. A Korean man was shivering during the flight and about to die on the airplane. The flight attendants called for doctors or nurses to help. So I went and saw him; he was shivering, shaking, and having problems breathing. He had a fever and cold sweat on the plane. I laid my hand on and prayed for him, and he started feeling calm and relaxed. His temperature went down to normal, and he got healed on the plane. The flight attendants were so thankful.

It was mid-December 2019 when we returned, and I realized the man probably had COVID. It already spread because so many Chinese people go to Thailand for vacations. We thank God for bringing us back to America safely and in good health.

Also, back home in Wisconsin, in November and December, the remaining people at our new church building in Green Bay had meetings to close the church because it was in an industrial zoning area, and not commercial. My older brother, who is our realtor, told us that once we bought it, we could have church services there. I told him that it was an industrial zone, and the city would not allow it, but he said he was an attorney and had the power to change anything. After we bought it, he didn't know what to do and the city told us to stop having church. The enemy worked through idolatry and demons on the mission field and used zoning regulations back home. Still, we remained focused on bearing fruit by preaching the gospel.

Now it happened on a certain day, as He was teaching, that there were Pharisees and teachers of the law sitting by, who had come out of every town of Galilee, Judea, and Jerusalem. And the power of the Lord was present to heal them. (Luke 5:17 NKJV)

²⁹ So Jesus answered and said, "Assuredly, I say to you, there is no one who has left house or brothers or sisters or father or mother or wife or children or lands, for My sake and the gospel's, ³⁰ who shall not receive a hundredfold now in this time— houses and brothers and sisters and mothers and children and lands, with persecutions—and in the age to come, eternal life. (Mark 10:29-30 NKJV)

Some initially mocked and ridiculed the healings in our ministry, but we have seen God heal people in so many nations that we are unmoved by mockery. God's power is present to heal when we obey His Word and go to the nations. We have fasted, prayed, suffered uncomfortable conditions, and been on adventures for the gospel's sake. And God has never failed us. He continues to provide supernaturally and will do the same for all who partner with him in gospel adventures.

CHAPTER 11: FRUITFULNESS AND PANDEMIC HEALINGS

On February 24, 2020, after many weeks of praying and fasting, the Lord directed us to have a final meeting and close the church in Green Bay. He directed us to move to Tulsa, OK, to build another church where the sick and demonized could come and stay to get healing, deliverance, and teaching. It would also be a place to worship God, fellowship, and teach and train disciples of Jesus Christ to harvest more souls for God's kingdom. It would be a center of communication and teaching via the Internet to reach people all over the world to know Jesus and be saved. We had been going to the nations, but God had given us a vision for a center to equip others to go.

***

In the Summer of 2020, I heard the phone ring.

> "Hello, brother. How are you?" I answered. A troubled voice replied.

> "Things are pretty bad right now," he sighed.

> "What's going on?"

> "Well . . . our church stayed open. But now we have several members who have gotten COVID, and I have been very sick. At times I cannot even breathe. I've had to go to the emergency room many times. We believe God can heal this thing. Will you come and pray for me and our church? I will

talk to my pastor and ask him to have you come to our church."

"Yes, we will stand with you. God can heal."

That call was from a brother in Christ in Mesa, Arizona at a predominantly white church in November of 2020 during the height of the pandemic.

Many pastors and church leaders were troubled during that time. Some were so perplexed and confused that all they knew to do was close their churches. Others brave enough to stay open had to deal with the potential for their members to get sick. For this brother's church, many of their members were sick and experiencing other health issues like arthritis, bodily pain, and aches, depression, and various organ diseases, so he asked me to come and minister.

When we got there, the glory of God came. The power of God touched their lives so strongly that many could not stand. One white woman had severe, chronic hip and knee pain and was on medication, but it wasn't helping. The power of God touched her. When she got up, she was healed. She didn't feel any more pain.

God touched so many others who were there. Although they were believers, the enemy still tried to oppress and torment them, but God's power was there to heal them.

Next, we went to an African American church in Phoenix, Arizona.

***

"Lord, I'm supposed to preach today. Should I go to this meeting and miss my preaching engagement? What am I supposed to do?" she asked.

"Go," the Spirit said. "I have shown you the vision."

"Okay, Lord. I'm going."

This woman preacher was having difficulty walking due to arthritis in her knees. She was preaching in pain, and God directed her to the meeting where we were preaching that day. She got healed right away and was overjoyed.

"Where are the people like you that God has given the gift of healings? I am healed," she shouted as she began to jump.

There were so many healings in that service. We were there for two days in Arizona. Everybody was so excited. Demons and sicknesses left, people received the Holy Spirit, spoke in tongues, and had their lives changed forever.

We continued to see miracles everywhere, whether in Asia, Africa, or the Midwest United States. God can heal all kinds of people and sicknesses everywhere—including COVID. We continued to travel during COVID. The airports were empty for a while, and airfare was the cheapest we had ever seen. There was one flight where it was just Tsee and I and one other couple on the entire plane. It felt like the world was a ghost town. It was a strange time, but God continued to touch lives.

> *. . . and the power of the Lord was present to heal them. (Luke 5:17b KJV)*

***

We continued to see God's mighty hand move throughout the pandemic. In March of 2021, we traveled to Nepal. Flying through the mountains in Nepal may sound beautiful, but this mountain was steep, and the flight was anything but comfortable or pleasant. It was the kind of flight that makes your stomach feel like it's fallen to your feet. Looking out the window, we felt we could touch the rocky cliffs. We had to brace ourselves for the turbulence and the narrow, dangerous landing the pilot would have to navigate, and we also were about to see the turbulence of God's power shake that mountain.

> "Hey everyone, this preacher from America, he will pray for you, and Jesus will heal you. Bring all the sick," the pastor said.

> "Okay . . . two or three people come up here. I will pray for you before I preach." I shouted.

A few people came forward, and the rest of the crowd of over 1,000 people from various villages watched intently. Most of them were idol worshipers and wore traditional clothes that made the crowd look like a sea of red, bright colors. Many of them had walked six or eight hours (the whole day) to get there, and when they saw the first few miracles with their own eyes, that was it! We didn't know they were Mongolians who were Genghis Khan's descendants.

The more they listened to us preach about the Gospel of Jesus Christ—His death, burial, and resurrection—the more they believed. They were so excited to hear John 3:16. They saw that Jesus was more powerful than their gods through the miracles and healings. The gospel was preached and demonstrated, so faith had been ignited. When I said, "Okay, who would like to give their life to Jesus Christ," for the first time, over five hundred people who lived on that mountain raised their hands. They wanted to know Jesus and give their lives to Him. It was glorious!

After preaching, I prayed for more people, demons started to flee, and many people fell to the ground in response to the power of God. These were not "churched" people. They were genuinely responding to God's delivering power, and they got up, healed and delivered.

The pastor who invited us had faith and wanted to see his people healed. He had seen some of our miracle videos on Facebook and asked us to come to his country to help pray for the sick. We had never been to Nepal but told him we would pray. We fasted and sought God about it, and He opened the door for us to go. The pastor was full of faith and excitement. He told everyone in the villages on the mountain, "Bring all the sick," and they did. They brought the sick from every village on the mountain to that outdoor crusade. While the rest of the world was focused on a "global pandemic," over 1,000 people walked down the valley and up the mountain, hoping to be healed. God did not disappoint them.

Next, we went down the mountain to a local village church. The pastor there said only a few people were filled with the Holy Spirit with the evidence of speaking in tongues. He only knew of a few in the entire country. We were shocked. So we taught about the Holy Spirit in his church, and people began to receive the Holy Spirit in Jesus' name. They repented of their sins and received the Holy Spirit. Men and women—everyone started speaking in tongues and receiving the Holy Spirit. It was a mighty move of God's Spirit. Afterward, their lives were changed. Alcohol addictions were gone. Smoking addictions were gone. Those who were about to divorce reconciled. Anger and depression were gone. People were just free—where the Spirit of the Lord is, there is liberty (2 Corinthians 3:17). It was an amazing and powerful move at that little church of about seventy people, and it was near a Buddhist temple.

Buddhist temples were everywhere in Nepal. It's like approximately a 90% Buddhist nation. Hinduism is also widespread, with temples on every corner around the few churches.

How then shall they call on him in whom they have not believed? and how shall they believe in him of whom they have not heard? and how shall they hear without a preacher? (Romans 10:14 KJV)

After we returned to the States from Nepal in April of 2021, we continued to go. This time, in October we went to Sweden and France.

In Sweden, the weather was always cloudy and gloomy, and the people there were just as gloomy and depressed. Sweden has a high rate of suicide; it is a stronghold for the people of Sweden. On the day of the meeting at the church, many people came demonized, sick, and depressed, but they were all delivered, healed, and set free from evil spirits. God allowed me to see these spirits when it was time to cast them out. It was a mighty move of God.

In France, we went to two cities. The first church was Bourge, which is south of Paris. All who came to the altar were saved, healed, and delivered. Then we went to Nimes in southern France by the Mediterranean Sea. Many who came were saved, healed, delivered, received the Holy Spirit, and began to speak in tongues. A young man who had dislocated his shoulder drove three hours to meet us at the revival. He was in severe pain and came into the meeting crying in pain. I anointed his right shoulder with water from the Mediterranean Sea, where the Apostle Paul had been shipwrecked, and he was instantly healed. He could move his arm in a normal range of motion without pain. Everyone was amazed. Glory to God!

Prophecy Manifested

It has been amazing and such a blessing for us to go to many different nationalities and denominations to minister the gifts and see people freed from Satan's bondages to God's peace, love, and freedom.

In 2014, Peter Yang said, "You will be the first Hmong Evangelist to go to many nations and preach the good news of Jesus, and to heal and deliver many people from darkness to light to God's side." "God has chosen you out of millions of people to do His will. Be glad, because someday I will be calling you older brother."

And this gospel of the kingdom shall be preached in all the world for a witness unto all nations; and then shall the end come. (Matthew 24:14 KJV)

God has given us so many testimonies, and they are not slowing down. We continue to see God open doors to the nations.

The Sword, the Serpent, and the Spiritual Realm

***

In January 2022, we went to Guayaquil, Ecuador, in South America, to minister in six churches there. The seventh church was about five hours away, up high in the mountains where the indigenous people called "Incas" lived. About 99 % of them still worshipped idols.

The six churches we visited in Guayaquil and the surrounding areas were filled with miracles. Hundreds of people were saved, healed, and delivered. They had never seen anything like it before. Our driver was an atheist, but after three days of being with us, he was convinced and gave his life to Jesus.

The scenery up the mountain where the Inca people lived was beautiful. They still wore traditional clothing and planted crops like the old days along the steep mountainside. All who came to the altar during these meetings were saved, healed, and delivered in Jesus' name. Eighteen idol worshippers were saved. A woman came to the altar in pain, but when I placed a towel over her body and took it off, she was healed instantly (Acts 19:12).

In June 2022, we went to an African American church in Minneapolis, MN, and then to a White church in Milwaukee, WI, and saw many incredible miracles. The church in Minneapolis had stopped doing church since the beginning of 2020 because of the pandemic. But after we went, they opened for the first time since then. The anointing was so great that people fell down as I approached them, their sicknesses left, and worries gone in Jesus' name. The family of a senator from Minnesota came and received healing. Glory to God.

Next, we went to a Hispanic church in Arkansas. Again, I used my hands to fight like a sword at every meeting since 2016, which the Lord taught me in my dreams to do (Psalm 144:1) and to blow air out of my mouth (Genesis 2:7, John 20:22) and speak the Word of God through revelation, knowledge, wisdom, and taking action by faith. Miracles came, and people were freed and healed in Jesus' name. We also went to Alaska again in June and saw many miracles.

In the summer of 2022, Thai military leaders invited us to minister. A Thai admiral in charge of all the government's warships invited us to minister in a government church in Bangkok. That is unheard of because many government churches don't allow the true gospel.

Then, another Thai general who controlled about 15,000 soldiers invited us to another government church to preach and pray for the sick in the province of Nan. The last general was in Chiang Mai, near the border of Myanmar. It's a church for the army, air force, navy, police, and other authorities who believe in God. In Thailand, 92.5% are Buddhist, 5.4 are Muslim, and 1.2 are Christians. There, idol worshipers gave their lives to Jesus Christ. Many were saved, healed, and delivered, and there were many miracles. There was a dead baby that we prayed for in 2018 that came back to life. Now that she was bigger, her parents brought her to meet us at the hotel. God is still working miracles! We went to eight Thai, Hmong, and Lasu churches in all. Also, we drove two hours up the mountain where many Idol worshippers gave their lives to Jesus, and all were healed in His name. Glory to God!

We also traveled to India near the China border in October of 2022. There were about 15,000 people in that meeting, and hundreds of people gave their lives to Jesus Christ. The next day, more people came to Jesus; His power delivered and healed them. Some police officers came to the meeting secretly to spy, and they were not happy that people were getting saved, so they tried to arrest us. We fled, lost our luggage, and hid for two nights and days.

We got away and went to Communist Laos to preach there. It was the first time in history that we had a chance to go to the biggest church there. The leader allowed us to preach but said no missionaries were allowed to preach outside; it had to be an indoor meeting. We agreed, and there were still so many salvations, healings, miracles, and water baptisms.

In June 2023, my wife and I went to Long Island, New York, to an African American church. The outpouring of the Holy Spirit was so strong—everyone at the meeting got healed and delivered in Jesus' name. The next day, about six people were water-baptized. Praise the Lord!

We returned to Hiroshima, Japan, and Thailand to minister in six churches, one of which was a government church and another a Catholic church. We were also invited to the biggest church in the world, Yoido Full Gospel Church, founded by Pastor David Yonggi Cho, to visit their church and sleep at their prayer mountain. Dr. Kim, the president and main pastor, met us, took us to lunch, and came very early in the morning to greet us before we left South Korea. We went to another church in Korea to pray for the sick and do deliverance. Many were healed and delivered instantly in Jesus' name.

Then we returned to Thailand to minister in six churches in six towns and saw so many people, especially idol worshippers, saved, healed, and delivered from demons in Jesus' name. The way God uses me as His instrument to minister to people is unique and different from many other ministers on earth (see videos on YouTube under Salad Vang, Ephesians 2:10). I thank God every day that He uses me as His servant to preach the gospel with the power to save, heal, and deliver nations in Jesus' name.

Some people have asked me why I see more miracles overseas than in the United States. One reason is those overseas who need miracles don't have a backup plan. They don't have credit cards, money, or insurance to see a doctor. They are poor; they can't buy medicine or see a doctor. So if your ministry and church services don't give relief or demonstrate God's power and blessings, they are going to die, and they know it. They don't have any backup plans. They come with faith to the altar; they come believing with everything on the inside of them.

When you say, "God can do it." They start saying, "God can do it; God can do it." That's why there are more miracles overseas than in developed countries like the USA. They have faith without a backup plan. They know what they are doing. They say, "If I don't get it here, I'm gonna die. I'm gonna do it, so I'm gonna get it here, now." And they get results. In America, you hear things like, "Please pray for me. Tomorrow, I'm going to the hospital." That's not desperation for the miracle of God that is available through faith.

I have learned that we need to have faith in the voice of God and the Word of God. When the Lord speaks to you, and you get a clear direction from God, do it. Our greatness manifests when we learn to trust in God (Proverbs 3:5-6) and work towards doing His will. God cannot use us if we are unmovable and unwilling to go. So get up and do something—take action. There's a time for praying and asking, but there's a time for getting up and taking action to do the will of God. It takes faith to do that. We have done that so many times by going to nations with the threat of police, demonic attacks, and dangerous terrain. God protected us while everyone around us was sick with COVID-19, and it did not even touch us. We never got sick during our trips. Glory to God.

Our lives are evidence of the powerful things God can do with people others do not expect Him to use. I was an atheist who did not want my wife to associate with believers. He radically changed our lives and opened our eyes to the spiritual realm. Now, He is using us to impact nations. We have seen such fruitfulness—salvations, healings, deliverances, miracles. Glory to God! He can open big doors when you walk in faith, and by His grace, we will continue to go to the nations. We pray that others will join us and live out their kingdom assignments in boldness and faith for kingdom adventures.

He said to them, "Go into all the world and preach the gospel to all creation. [16] Whoever believes and is baptized will be saved, but

whoever does not believe will be condemned. [17] And these signs will accompany those who believe: In my name they will drive out demons; they will speak in new tongues; [18] they will pick up snakes with their hands; and when they drink deadly poison, it will not hurt them at all; they will place their hands on sick people, and they will get well."
(Mark 16:15-18 NIV)

About the Author

Salad Vang was born in Long Cheng, Laos, of the Hmong people, who were long-standing Shamanist idol worshippers. In 1975, his family fled the communist invasion of Laos and lived in a Thailand refugee camp until they came to America in 1980.

After coming to America, he worked hard to pursue an education and obtained a B.Sc. degree in 1995, a Doctor of Chiropractic degree in 2001, and a Doctor of Medicine degree in 2008. But while his business was thriving, his marriage was not. His wife, Tsee, had grown weary of their extravagant, worldly lifestyle and was fasting and praying for him to receive Christ. A year after their daughter suffered from seizures and went into a coma, God answered Tsee's prayers, and Salad received Christ as his Lord and Savior.

A few days later, Salad and Tsee had the same dream through which the Lord revealed the source of the witchcraft that had attacked their marriage and caused their daughter's sickness. Afterward, they prayed to God to heal their daughter and saw two tall angels, each holding a golden sword. Suddenly, two dark, small demonic spirits came out of their daughter, and she was healed immediately. *That was the beginning of their spiritual journey and realization of Jesus' supremacy over other gods.*

Vang went from being a skeptical evolutionary doctor to a believer in Christ Jesus who has preached to millions across the globe. His life transformed, and he now serves Jesus, dedicating his whole life to the Lord, Jesus Christ, and the healing and deliverance that only comes in His name.

For more information:

- Facebook: https://www.facebook.com/salad.vang1
- YouTube: https://www.youtube.com/@saladvanghealingofallnatio6197
- Twitter: @Salad Vang

www.ingramcontent.com/pod-product-compliance
Lightning Source LLC
Chambersburg PA
CBHW060839050426
42453CB00008B/752